Skip Tracing
Basics & Beyond

A Complete Step-by-Step Guide
for Locating Hidden Assets Second Edition

Susan Nash

iUniverse, Inc.
Bloomington

Skip Tracing Basics and Beyond
A Complete, Step-by-Step Guide for Locating
Hidden Assets Second Edition

iUniverse books may be ordered through booksellers or by contacting:

iUniverse
1663 Liberty Drive
Bloomington, IN 47403
www.iuniverse.com
1-800-Authors (1-800-288-4677)

Because of the dynamic nature of the Internet, any web addresses or links contained in this book may have changed since publication and may no longer be valid. The views expressed in this work are solely those of the author and do not necessarily reflect the views of the publisher, and the publisher hereby disclaims any responsibility for them.

Any people depicted in stock imagery provided by Thinkstock are models, and such images are being used for illustrative purposes only.

Certain stock imagery © Thinkstock.

ISBN: 978-1-4759-5756-3 (sc)
ISBN: 978-1-4759-5837-9 (e)
ISBN: 978-1-4759-5755-6 (dj)

Library of Congress Control Number: 2012920031

Printed in the United States of America

iUniverse rev. date: 11/07/2012

To my children, Eric and Jessica, who have always said to me, "You should write a book." I love you both more than you'll ever know.

And to my wonderful father, who has always been there for me no matter what. I sometimes think about how I may not have even existed if he hadn't escaped from Hitler. He is a miracle at eighty-seven, and I love him dearly.

And to my favorite aunt Resi, who has supported me throughout my life especially in my times of need. I had valuable secrets passed down to me about surviving from Hitler. Her eighty-five years of wisdom is one of my most valuable assets.

Contents

Author's Note

After getting my baccalaureale degree in accounting from Queens College, and while studying for my CPA exam, I decided to take a step back and look at myself from the outside in. What did I see? What was I to do with all this knowledge I had just obtained? How could I best use that information to serve both my personal satisfaction and needs and give back by serving our society? I examined different avenues to use my skills and feel satisfied at a personal level. I knew I was talented and gifted in many areas and disciplines, and I wanted a way to incorporate all those skills together so I could be of service and give back.

I started to investigate career options to see what type of work would keep me interested for the long term. All sorts of paths turned me on—some were more labor intensive, some were more capital intensive, and some were more intellectually intensive. Each had its ups and downs, or pros and cons, but one captured my heart. Believe it or not, I found an initial niche in the business of serving judicial judgments or court orders. The pivotal moment that turned me in that direction was that it was my chance to right a wrong for someone else. After looking into this somewhat arcane field, I discovered that it was such a huge and vastly infinite opportunity with so many possibilities that I just couldn't resist the urge to get involved.

My friends, relatives, and counselors were against the idea. Some said, "Are you serious? Are you for real?" I told everyone that I was 100 percent serious and that I wanted to try my hand at something unique. Let's face it. Not everybody thinks serving legal papers or tracking down deadbeats is the way to a fantastic career. It is sort of thinking outside the box, isn't it?

I did my homework. I discovered that the business had all the elements to keep my adrenaline going, and it was a natural high. Against everyone's advice and better judgment, I followed my heart. Almost twenty years ago, I founded Search-Net Management, a company that locates assets to satisfy judgments. Before you can locate assets, you have to figure out where to search for them, and that's how my expertise as a skip tracer first took root. Skip tracing became a fundamental part of my job. It was so important that without knowing how to skip trace I could never succeed.

When I began working in this field, I had no idea of the number of times I would encounter people who were interested in earning their living doing the same thing. It seems I was not (and am not) alone in my interest in this profession. Lots of people approached me, asking for advice and guidance. I remember when I first became interested that I looked for books on the topic, and I found almost none. I always felt that more material was needed, so I began developing the basis of this guide to the basics of skip tracing that I shared with other people over the years.

One thing led to another, and I began working with people like you, people who want to learn the profession of skip tracing, or those of us already in the field who want to get additional tips. Through my business at Search-Net Management, I have trained hundreds of individuals, and I have worked with such organizations as the National Business Institute (www.nbi-sems.com), and the Institute for Paralegal Education (IPE), teaching a yearly Skip Tracing seminar. You can trust the National Business Institute and the Institute for Paralegal Education with your continuing education needs. Quite simply, they are the best! They are a loved and trusted source provider to the continuing education market. They have been the largest provider of legal and professional education in the country for over a quarter of a century. They have trained over two million professionals. When you train with them, not only do you make an investment in your career, but you also make an investment in yourself.

Additional resources and seminar formats let you customize your educational experience. Many online seminars can be found at WestLegalEdCenter.com. When working online, you'll be able to enjoy the same great quality as our live seminars, all from the convenience of your office or home. In-house, customizable, convenient, and cost-efficient seminars can be brought to your facility on a schedule that works for you. Previously held NBI and IPE seminars are available for purchase as audio, CDs, and written reference manuals. Reference manuals can be purchased in three different formats, including a downloadable PDF file that's immediately accessible via the website. Many of our clients request the seminar brochure in an electronic format because it is a convenient and effective method of obtaining the information.

I have been skip tracing for almost twenty years, and I feel that I have become a master hunter. I have the confidence and know how to be able to demonstrate how to do it correctly, efficiently, and effectively without huge outlays of capital or energy. I assure you that you will benefit by picking up new resources to find exactly what you need, and the research techniques to make it nice and easy.

Enter the fascinating world of skip tracing, and discover a potentially rewarding and lucrative career, just like I did!

—Susan Nash

Introduction

Life can be strange. We all know that's the case, and for some of us, life can be really strange. If a criminal defrauds you and gets out of town fast, that's strange and annoying. You want to track the guy down and get your money back, if you can. That's true for individuals and companies. If a loved one dies and leaves everything in order except for a mysterious key that might open up a box of hidden assets, that's mystifying (and definitely annoying too). You want to know what box that key unlocks, right? You want to know what's in the box! Correct?

Of course!

The question is how do you get the information you want and need? You could call in a private investigator to help. Or you could call in a more specialized searcher to ferret out the truth. You could call someone like me—a professional skip tracer. Although the term doesn't come up on crime shows on TV, in the rarified circles within the intelligence community that I have moved in for nearly two decades, a skip tracer is the person who comes up with the gold when everything else seems to be nothing but straw. We know how to find people who don't want to be found—the skips—and we know how to get the answers your clients want and need, all within the confines of the law and ethics.

What is a skip? We'll get into that in more detail later, but for our purposes right now, let's just say a skip can be a deadbeat who has run off, leaving loads of debt behind. Basically, he or she is a career fraudster. The skip is missing in action, and there's no way to get in touch with him or her to collect the money. A skip can be someone who left town without knowing a bill had not been paid, and who had no nefarious intentions in mind. Skips can be criminals, but they can also be innocent people who don't even know they're classified as skips. Skips can be dead people. Like the guy who died and left a key to a safety deposit box his family didn't know about, a safety deposit box that he shared with his mistress. Believe me, I've seen it all. Like people, skips come in all shapes and sizes and types. In the end, though, a skip is a skip, and as a pro skip tracer (or skip chaser), it's up to you to track the skip down and resolve the case for your client.

The art of skip tracing has been around since biblical times. A classic example of this would be the biblical figure Delilah, who seduced Samson, discovered the secret of his strength, and sold it to the enemy. She essentially skipped with his vulnerabilities, which ultimately led to his demise. As times evolved, so did intelligence styles. What once took a gumshoe weeks of investigating to obtain can now be had in minutes with a simple phone call, or in seconds on your computer or mobile device. Today we do business using additional, new and improved techniques and technologies. Things change quickly, including espionage standards and strategies. The web is dynamic and is an ever-changing medium; it changes every minute of every day. As this book goes to press, there is a renewed emphasis on skip tracing methods that comply with privacy laws. The financial world is starting to see skip tracing as a value-added element in the big picture, and as a would-be or practicing skip tracer yourself, you don't want to be left out.

Skip tracing is changing fast in the intelligence world. As I've said, skip tracing helps businesses and individuals find people that cannot be easily located, or who do not want to be found. People go missing for all kinds of reasons. Sometimes people marry and move away and change their names. Sometimes people divorce and do not want to be found because they owe child support or alimony. Sometimes individuals leave because they are being looked for to repossess their car. There are so many reasons people try to disappear, and we will get into those in later chapters. My point is that skip tracing is a real asset in a wide variety of industries. In fact, I'd argue that every industry category requires expert skip tracers.

Let's say you are a Realtor. You might need to find who owns a property you are interested in selling. You would need to hire a skip tracer to find that information. If you can't find the owner of the house, you won't be able to sell the house and make a commission. Since that is how real estate brokers make a living, it is vital that they find a way to obtain that information. In fact, some businesses would lose a fortune without being able to get the information they need. The benefit of skip tracing is that without it there would be no profit. With a small investment in skip tracing, clients reap a huge return on a minimal investment. It is so important, that some industries can't function without skip tracers.

This book is a must for anyone considering a career as a skip tracer, or for anyone in the field already but who wants to pick up some great tips. This book is also designed for attorneys, collection agencies, estate planning, family law, banking, lenders, creditors, factors, financial personnel, paralegals, private investigators, process servers, security personnel, researchers, information brokers, data brokers, snoops, litigators, credit and collections professionals, debt buyers, auditors, accountants, tax professionals, law enforcement, property managers, personal injury work, genealogists, probate matters, and real estate personnel. *Skip Tracing Basics and Beyond* is a valuable resource for anyone interested in participating in these fields.

Being an effective skip tracer isn't easy. It takes knowledge and tenacity. You've got to know what to do, and that's where this book comes in. For example, proper behavior in investigative settings can be a scary topic. Being unsure of what move to make or what move should come next is often quite unnerving. When we're scared, we don't think very well. That can make successful interaction seem almost impossible. Some people fall down under pressure. If you fall, you'll need to pick yourself up and dust yourself off and do it all over again.

As a skip tracer, you'll be faced with all kinds of situations that require a basic knowledge of the law, and a basic knowledge of how to outfox the skip. Ask yourself the following questions:

- What exactly is the difference between a legal pretext and an illegal pretext?

- When I'm skip tracing, what should I say or avoid saying?

- How do I handle people who come across too strong?

- What will the new standard for the twenty-first century be?

You need to know the answers to these questions, and you'll find them in this book. As I've said, I've met many people who are eager, as you are, to learn how to skip trace legally and ethically. It's important that we professionals understand how to conduct ourselves properly so that we comply with all the laws on a state and federal level. Anyone who wants to be a skip tracer, private investigator, or researcher, or anyone who has a need to get the information for his or her own use will find this book an essential guide to skip tracing basics. In these pages, you will learn the top skip-tracer secrets, and all of them are 100 percent legal.

Here's a sneak peek at one of the secrets you'll be privy to: How can you tell when you are in a room, restroom, motel room, restaurant, gym, locker room, changing room, bathroom, fitting room, and other such places whether a mirror is a two-way glass? Here's how—I thought it was quite interesting! And I know in about thirty seconds you're going to do what I did and find the nearest mirror. A policewoman who travels all over the United States and gives seminars and techniques for businesswomen passed this on to the NCISS president, who in turn passed it on to one of the women's Yahoo! Groups, and I have just passed it on to you. How many of you know for sure whether the seemingly ordinary mirror hanging on the wall is a real mirror or is actually a two-way mirror (they can see you, but you can't see them)? There have been many cases of people installing two-way mirrors in female changing rooms. It is very difficult to positively identify the surface by looking at it. So, how do you determine with any amount of certainty what type of mirror you are looking at? Just conduct this simple test: Place the tip of your fingernail against the reflective surface. If there is a *gap* between your fingernail and the image of the nail, then it is a *genuine* mirror. However, if your fingernail *directly touches* the image of your nail, then *beware! It is a two-way mirror!* So remember, every time you see a mirror, do the "fingernail test." It doesn't cost you anything. Remember: no space, leave the place!

The specific applications presented in this book reinforce the basic principles in ways that you can easily use. When you know you're doing the right thing and recognize how to do it, you feel more confident, are better informed, and are better prepared for the challenges that come your way during the skip tracing process. There are challenges every step of the way, and we will get to those in more detail later on. Just like there are challenges in life every day, there are challenges in skip tracing, but none are too big that we cannot overcome them. When it becomes so natural that you don't need to think about your every move or word is when you begin to feel some self-confidence and allow your instinctive nature to show itself.

If you are a skip tracer, you need to recognize that your subject may be a career criminal and may be hiding in camouflage so you won't see him or recognize him. There is a principle of duality in everything we do. Every coin has two sides; for every action, there is an equal and opposite reaction. Everything can be seen from two sides. Never confuse education with intelligence, and never confuse intelligence with education. What is the "norm" is not the norm in skip tracing. Cop mistakes son for intruder or son mistakes cop for intruder. These are the types of challenges that might seem intimidating at first, but you will learn to navigate through the obstacles with your eyes clearly on the goal.

Let *Skip Tracing Basics and Beyond* be your guide into a world few of us ever get to see. The concrete advice you will find in these pages will help you in specific situations that you are likely to encounter as a professional skip tracer, providing you with the knowledge you need to conduct your investigations more effectively and with more confidence, know-how, and efficiency than ever before. Little things really do mean a lot. In short, this book will help you use your *tools* to work for you, instead of *you* working for your tools.

Chapter 1
Skip Tracing 101

Choose a job you love, and you will never have to work a day in your life.

—Confucius

Let's start with the basics and work from there. We'll define the nature of skip tracing and what it takes to be a successful skip tracer. Then we'll take a look at the various types of skips, and at the art of tracking skips down. In the collection and investigative industries, any debtor whose current address and place of employment is unknown is referred to as a *skip.* The term *skip* is applied to a debtor who cannot be readily located by usual, routine methods. A skip is someone who you have no way of reaching, either by phone or by mail. The term comes from the idiomatic expression "to skip town," meaning to depart, perhaps in a rush, and leave no clues behind for anyone to trace the skip to a place. *Skip tracing* is the art of obtaining information about someone who doesn't want to be found.

Successful Skip Tracers
Share Common Traits

Skip tracing is an art and not a science. There is no black or white. There is no magic formula or set of procedures. One important characteristic is to be quick-thinking and ready for anything, because after we place a call, we never know who will pick up on the other side. Unlock the creative powers of your mind. Use your intuition and insight. Remember to use common sense and to be original.

Skip tracing as an art can be compared with mind-set and sport. Do you have what it takes to be a successful skip tracer? Do you have the right personality for the skip tracing profession? It requires strength and perseverance. Some characteristics and traits of a successful skip tracer include intelligence, common sense, patience, friendly personality, persistence, detail orientation, assertiveness, persuasion, creativity, competitiveness, and goal orientation.

While there is no degree given to a skip tracer, many states do have educational requirements and those vary from state to state. Some states require a private investigator's license, and some states require that you go to school and then pass a state exam. Some states like New York do not require that you attend school, but in order to be a private investigator, the state requires that you work as an apprentice under someone else's license for a period of at least three years before you can go out and practice on your own. Many colleges around the country teach skip tracing classes as part of a criminal college curriculum and degree. But there is no degree that is given for the sole purpose of skip tracing. Many states also have a continuing education requirement for private investigators, but that also varies from state to state. There are no federal guidelines as of yet because these are regulated at the state level.

People often get set in their ways, and this book is meant to help you expand your mind. Think about a horse running on a racetrack. One piece of equipment the horse has to help him is his blinders. They are designed to make the horse look straight ahead and not be distracted by anything outside of the course and his line of vision. Now if we take his blinders off, we have expanded his line of vision because he can look all around. Take off your blinders and look at the bigger picture. This concept is called *expanding your parameters*.

Expanding Your Parameters Allows You to See the Big Picture

Avoiding tunnel vision is essential in successful skip tracing. *Tunnel vision* is a condition in which a person lacks any peripheral vision. It is caused by, among other things, information being presented in small fragments not related to their context. This results in a constricted, circular, tunnel-like field of vision, similar to looking through a peephole. Sometimes when we are skip tracing, instead of opening our eyes and minds, we get stuck in a certain perspective and cannot react fast enough. Sometimes we might get stuck and not see clearly. This might cause us to see things in a warped or twisted way, and we want to make sure we always focus on the bigger picture. Try to see things as if you were an outsider looking in. I sometimes like to think of myself as a bird flying around above the territory where my skip should be, and then I try to look from above and see a different view. Almost as if the bird were hunting a victim for food. It is mind over matter.

While many refer to skip tracing as an art, a mind-set, and a sport, you must not lose sight of your ultimate goal, which is to find that someone who doesn't want to be found. You will make your living ferreting out sneaks and creeps who would rather not be found. One approach that is often used is to step into the shoes of that skip and think like that person would think. The skip will most likely try to mislead you. Try to stay one or two steps ahead of them; many of them are masters of deception.

Skip tracing is the ability to think through and analyze the circumstances of each situation individually in order to reach our goals. Good organizational skills play a fundamental part in maximizing our time and resources in order to improve our performance. Time management and deadlines are factors that will affect our effectiveness, so having a strategy will prove most efficient. Tactics are the specific actions, sequences of actions, and schedules you use to fulfill your strategy. If you have more than one strategy, you will have different tactics for each. Plan for attaining a particular goal by having detailed maneuvers to achieve your objectives set by strategy—just like a game of chess.

Your actions must seem natural and executed with ease. All the hard work and practice that goes into them, including the clever tricks, must be hidden. When you act, act effortlessly, as if you do much more. Avoid the temptation of revealing how hard you work—it only raises questions. Keep your tricks sealed in your bag of tricks and tap into the fantasies that people flock to. Keep all your statistical forecasts and probability ratios stored away so that when you need to use a trick, you can just look inside your bag and see which one will be most appropriate to get what you need. Mathematical and psychological profiling will also come in handy when you need to create some magic. We will discuss some more of these techniques later. Skip tracing is slow and gradual. It requires hard work, a bit of luck, some self-sacrifice—and a lot of patience. Never be in a hurry. Become a detective of the right moment and sniff out the spirit of the time and the trends that will carry you to reach realization.

Skips Come in All Shapes and Sizes

Profiling and categorizing the various types of skips will have a profound effect on your results. My rational is that once you know what type of skip you are looking for, you will immediately know what direction to take your research without wasting time on leads that don't fit your skip. I have had the opportunity to teach and work with people from every profession. Profiling and categorizing are some of the most valuable tricks the skip tracer uses to save time and plan effectively. Categorizing is one of the most important processes to consider when setting up the steps you will take to locate your skip.

There are three major skip categories: unintentional, convenient, and intentional. In addition, there are various subcategories of intentional skips that we will discuss in detail.

Unintentional Skip: This person might not know he's missing. These types are most commonly found in missing heirs cases, unclaimed property, and missing witnesses. People in this category will usually be rewarded when found, instead of punished. These are usually the easiest skips to locate.

Convenient Skip: This type of skip most likely knows he is missing and has conveniently failed to notify the client that he has moved. People in this group do not go to great lengths to cover their current location. Usually they are easy to locate.

Intentional Skip: This person probably left his last known address because he is attempting to hide from your client. He disappeared for the exact reason you are attempting to find him. This category can be broken out further into three subcategories:

Soft-core intentional skip: This person is usually younger, and he is not that well informed on how to hide and can usually be found with little effort. A simple name search on Google could get you his address and phone number. We'll go into great length on using the Internet later. This might be a beginner or novice skip.

Hard-core intentional skip: This person is an experienced skip and has learned by his past mistakes. The most important lessons in life are the most expensive ones, and he has learned to camouflage. In general, he knows what to do to cover his tracks. However, like most, sooner or later he will slip and make a mistake, and you'll find him. Persistence is the key. Do it over and over till you get it right. Nothing will do the job as well as practice. You need to practice doing it till you achieve perfection, which is to locate the skip. This might be an intermediate or expert skip.

Intentional skip fraudsters: This person has a strong motivation to hide. He's usually a criminal or scammer who has several aliases and Social Security numbers. Sometimes these show up in Social Security number traces and are the most difficult locates. They can run, but they can't hide forever. The dogs eventually hunt them down. This might be an expert or professional skip.

The Most Common Types of Skips Are Easy to Identify

Now that we've looked at the broad categories of skips, let's zero in on the most common types you're likely to encounter.

Bail Bond Skips: Most bail bondsmen nationwide will sooner or later have a skip. He either does a subject locate or has to pay the amount of the bail to the court. If they don't know how to do it themselves, they often hire a bounty hunter who will work on a contingency fee, which can be several thousand dollars.

Missing Adoptees and Birth Parents: With adoption rates soaring, parents and children often search each other out later in life, which has often been quoted as a movement in the United States. These people will often hire skip tracers or missing persons investigators to locate their parent or child. You will find cases on both sides of the coin. Parents who placed a child for adoption will be looking for them, and children who know they are adopted might search out their natural parents.

Missing Family Members and Lost Loved Ones: With divorce rates continuing to be in the highest level in recent history and new extended families being formed and people moving all over the country and world to seek better and brighter futures, people will desire to connect with old friends, classmates, and family. Some will try to track them down, and they will often hire an information professional.

Tenant Skips: Landlord–tenant court filings are at an all-time high, and with the housing bubble bursting and the credit crunch affecting Americans nationwide, landlords find themselves with renters leaving several months of unpaid rent. Sometimes these skips abandon their former residence and leave a mess, causing the landlord to expend cash to get the dwelling back in shape to be able to rent it out again. These same problems have now extended into the commercial rental market in record numbers. Landlords and their attorneys usually turn to skip tracers to locate the skip.

Rental Agents: An industry which has more than doubled in size in the last ten years is the furniture, television, and electronic media rental business. Some of these categorize themselves as leasing companies. Although these rental companies charge premium prices for the rental of their goods, a big cost for them is the problems with the skips and the growing bad-debt expense ratios that deflect from their financial statements. People move away with their assets and cease paying the rental charges. In the past few years, television cable companies have been having the same problem with their equipment. These industries are turning to skip tracers to track down these people and repossess their merchandise.

Life Insurance Claimant Skips: When people move and don't notify their insurance company, the company gets returned mail, and it needs to locate their new address. The company needs to send out monthly premium notices that are being returned by the post office. If a policyholder disappears, a claim must be paid within a specified period if the person is not located or if fraud has not been committed. Insurance companies have hundreds of these cases on a monthly basis.

Lost Stockholders: Warehouses full of paperwork are stored to mine information about stockholders in the markets. In the age of electronic media and storage, the data must be stored. Many companies have decided to store backup data in storage facilities off the premises in order to protect themselves and have additional backup copies when needed in cases of theft or loss. Some criminals are so sophisticated that they are years ahead of most others. Cyber criminals are very smart; when they set their minds on something, they get it. Financial institutions generate a huge amount of this type of tracing work and are willing to pay a fee to a tracer to locate the missing investor.

Credit Card Charge-Offs: When credit card accounts fall into the delinquent category, and credit card issuers have no hope of collecting, they will need to locate the subject so that they can reduce the debt into a judgment. The lenders have a huge volume of this type of skip tracing work now because credit card delinquencies are at an all-time high. With the price of basic necessities increasing at a double-digit rate, many consumers are turning to credit cards to pay for basic items like food and groceries, gasoline, and other e-commerce-related purchases. In the last year alone, the price of bread has grown at the rate of 33 percent due to increased costs in the commodities. Consumers are using credit cards more than ever, and the charge-off rate is at the highest rate in history as well. With the charge-off rate expected to be at 35 percent, this will continue to be one of the fastest-growing areas. Please note that these percentage estimates are subjective; different media types report different findings, and the time differences also vary. These are ballpark figures.

Debt Buyer Skips: This is an industry that some say is reaching maturity, while others argue that it is just in the adolescent age. Because credit cards were only created in the 1950s, this is a relatively new industry in comparison with traditional debt instruments. Given the turmoil in the credit markets, these instruments are used as vehicles to generate revenue in a case where a loss will be incurred. Lenders only want to carry these on their books for so long. Although the raters' disastrous record in evaluating the soundness of the portfolios and other exotic financial instruments is well known, the financial markets love these instruments because they are so profitable. The buyers should perform a more direct examination method before purchasing them, and they sometimes use skip tracers to audit the portfolios. This is a recurring source of tracing work, because every quarter, decisions need to be made as to what to sell off. Hedge carefully.

Debtor Skips: When bank loans go bad, the lending institution will need to locate the note holder. Large banks have several different departments that have an ongoing need to locate these types of skips. The auto loan department generates a large volume of cases on a monthly basis seeking to repossess the vehicles to be able to auction them off in exchange for cash. The student loan departments, real estate loan departments, trust departments, probate departments, and returned check departments need skip tracers on a routine basis.

Judgment Debtor Skips: When businesses and individuals can't collect the money that is owed to them, they can either turn it over to the collection agency or they can go to court and get a judgment. Once the judgment has been awarded, the process of collecting is in a different ballpark and in a different league altogether. You have now expanded your resources and can garnish wages, levy on bank accounts, and lien on pensions. Locating judgment debtors is recession-proof because the worse the economy becomes, the more judgments that are awarded.

Unclaimed Property: This comes in all shapes and sizes. Some types of unclaimed properties are found in the form of stocks, bonds, bank accounts, investment accounts, insurance accounts, and deposit accounts with utility companies, phone companies, and cable companies. Skip tracers obtain lists of unclaimed property from state government agencies and then locate the missing owners for a profit. We will visit some websites later on.

Missing Heirs and Beneficiaries: When a will goes into probate court and family members contest the will, information professionals will need to trace safe deposit boxes, bank accounts, investment accounts, and other assets. These types of financial investigations are forensic in type and will often be used by the trustees of the estate. We'll get into more detail later on.

Missing Witnesses for Attorneys: Personal-injury attorneys need to locate witnesses to the incident in their caseloads. They usually outsource or hire an information broker to locate these subjects. Fees are usually charged at an hourly rate rather than a contingency fee. Other times, lawyers are confronted with a client who wants to bring legal action against another party who needs to be located for service of process.

Finding missing witnesses or heirs is a noble pursuit, and finding a deadbeat is just plain good justice! Can you see why someone would want to get into this business, especially if they're snooping to find an heir?

Providing Skip Tracing Services As an Independent Contractor for Companies and Private Investigators Can Be a Very Rewarding Career

Skip tracing and collections are two different skills, and clients should not mix them. Skip tracing is a specialty. Locating traceable items is a time-consuming and laborious process. Most business models can be painted, with broad brushstrokes, as a person with a head, hands, and feet. Skip tracers are the hands that do the work. The skip tracer and the collector are opposite personality types.

Personally, I would make a terrible collector—but I sure can locate! Hopefully we all know who we are and what our strengths and weaknesses are. If you know you're a good collector, stick to collections; if you're good at tracing, stick to tracing. I am a firm believer that we should build our strengths and compensate for our weaknesses. As you look for new business, emphasize the benefits you bring to the company. Make the point that skip tracing is a specialty, and that it makes no sense for the company to go outside its area of expertise and incur costs on search charges when outsourcing to you will cost nothing unless you get results.

Many collection agencies have their own in-house skip tracing departments. If you want to work for someone else, pursuing an in-house position could be an option for you. Many private investigators work for businesses that have in-house investigation departments and private investigators on staff. I have many clients that are private investigators who work for everything from insurance companies to personal injury attorneys. Some of them are extremely successful and have led exciting lives. Many of the private investigators specialize in one area, and most don't have a background in finance or in locating financial instruments and assets. That's where I come in.

The private investigators will usually call and say they have a case that is outside of their area of expertise and need to hire an expert in the financial area. This is when they outsource to skip tracers who specialize in locating people and assets. Private investigators and skip tracers usually specialize in one area or another just like doctors have specialties. There is the heart specialist, and there is the eye doctor. There is the oral surgeon, and the orthodontist. There are private investigators who work on probate cases, and those who work on auto repossessions. Because markets have become so segmented recently, it would be best to find your niche market by taking the first step and figuring out which field you love most. Your second step would be to investigate that market and see if that is your true calling. Your third step would be to go for it!

Here are a few additional points to make when pitching a potential client for his or her business:

- If your in-house skip tracers don't locate assets, why not turn to an outside source?

- An in-house skip tracer costs you a fixed amount for salary and other benefits. Sending cases out costs absolutely nothing unless they find what you want; if no assets are located, no cost will be incurred by the firm.

- By eliminating an in-house skip department, you are reducing your fixed costs for payroll expense, and you are reducing your variable costs in fee-based database charges.

- By outsourcing skips, you are bringing capital into your business and incurring no costs because the costs come out of the assets that have been located, and in many cases they are dead files that weren't going to yield any income anyway. Plus, the data comes prevalidated, so you save on verification costs, not to mention time and effort you should be spending on getting more cases. With electronic data transmissions, information that used to take weeks to prepare takes just seconds to transmit.

- Outsourcing your skip tracing is like sending work out on contingency. It provides more value to the client because it turns clutter into cash.

- It's critical to understand how much time a researcher needs to gather data in a trace. A "hand search" or manual search involves a person physically traveling to the source to review the information available. This process, when needed, is much more costly and time consuming. The whole process could be provided cost-free to the firm (if no assets are located), and it is ridiculously reliable.

It's important to note that many times the reason firms don't outsource the work is because the in-house staff that is currently doing the work needs to protect their job. They are usually the gatekeeper because management relies on their opinion, which is not necessarily in the best interest of the company or the client but is in the best interest of the person trying to protect their job. They don't want to look bad in front of management. From the standpoint of labor, outsourcing may represent a new threat, contributing to worker insecurity. Taking the long-term view means that eventually management will want to raise earnings and look at other options to increase profits, which will generally mean outsourcing to you.

Everything changes, so be strong and prosper.

The future belongs to those who believe in themselves.

—Eleanor Roosevelt

Chapter 2
Nabbing Debtor Skips

Yesterday is a canceled check; tomorrow is a promissory note; today is the only cash you have—so spend it wisely.

—Kay Lyons

Tracking down debtors is a big part of a skip tracer's job. That's the case because deadbeats who haven't paid their bills and have disappeared are the most common type of skips. Again, the skip could be unintentional, convenient, or intentional. Chances are the debtor skip is the intentional kind—soft-core, hard-core, or fraudster. It's also important to note that not all skips are individuals. Businesses can be skips too, and they can pose a real challenge. We'll talk about both kinds of debtors—individuals and corporations—within the context of skip tracing to get your clients the money they're owed. Another key issue we'll cover in this chapter is identity theft. I see such cases all the time when trying to track down a supposed debtor, only to find out the person I'm looking for doesn't exist, that he or she is a fabrication created out of some hapless victim of fraud.

Debtors Are the Most Common Type of Skip—and They Can Be People or Businesses

Let's discuss nabbing individual debtors first. The skip tracer is so important to the collection industry that it is almost impossible to collect without one. If you cannot locate your deadbeat, then you will not be able to collect. The skip tracer does not do the actual collection, but reports and works directly for the collector or the collection agency or the debt buyer. As every experienced collector knows, the odds of collecting a delinquent account improve substantially if you know where the debtor lives or works.

You should develop your strategy right at the start of the trace. Your first goal would be to locate the debtor and, hopefully, as a byproduct, get a phone number. Many people say that skip tracing is like solving a puzzle, and we should put all the pieces together to see the whole picture. That almost seems too scientific and preengineered, but you want to try to step into the shoes of the skip and figure out how he thinks, so that you can trace his steps and find the information to collect what is owed.

Intuition and insight are important techniques, and right at the start is when you should use them. Try closing your eyes for a second and see if you can get a "feel" for the debtor. What I mean by "feel" is not what they look like, but what type of person they are. Going just on instinct, see how many of these questions you can answer about the skip.

Do they have a job?

Are they a citizen, legal resident, or an illegal alien?

Are they on public assistance?

Are they blue-collar or white-collar?

Are they green-collar or pink-collar?

Are they public sector or private sector?

Could they be a government employee?

Are they a municipal, state, or federal employee?

Do they have a union job?

Are they self-employed?

What is the salary bracket?

Do they have a pension?

If they have a pension, how is it funded?

Are they vested?

Do they have insurance, and what kind?

Is it health, life, property, or casualty insurance?

Do they have a medical profile?

Are they bonded or licensed? If so, by whom and as what?

Are they computer literate?

Do they have a website? A domain name or an e-mail address?

Are they type A or type B personalities?

What are their hobbies?

Are they a spender or a saver?

Are they a gambler or a philanthropist?

Do they live in the mountains, on the ocean, near the lake, by the river, on an island, on a farm?

Do they live in the city or the suburbs?

Do they own any real property?

Is there any equity in the house?

Are they married or single?

Do they have kids? Are they natural or adopted children?

Do they have a car?

Is the car leased or purchased outright?

Is it paid for in cash or was it on credit?

Is it a revolving or an installment loan?

Does it have a guarantor?

Do they have other tangible assets such as boats, airplanes, tractors, livestock, tools, motorcycles, art, jewelry, minerals, or antiques?

Once you get a feel for the person, plan your next step. Different people have different personalities. If your debtor is a new mother, she will not be traveling all over the world. Generally speaking, she would live a more tranquil kind of life, and her routine would be around a newborn baby who needs to feed and nap many times a day. Think about the needs for her baby and her schedule. She probably needs to buy diapers and formula and baby products. This will give you an idea of the type of life that she is living. You might need to follow her to find out what ATM machine she uses to get cash or how she transacts business. Does she get food stamps or public assistance?

The new mother as a debtor type would be very different from a pilot who is always on the run and traveling internationally. We would use two different approaches to find each one. It might be very difficult to follow a pilot if he was all over the world, so we would need to use two different methods for each one. Once you know what type of debtor you have, it will be easier to determine which kinds of assets they will have. An international pilot who travels the world might have different assets that he deals with because he may be importing or exporting them. It would be more probable that he has assets overseas. First, determine what kinds of assets the debtor has, so you can trace the infamous paper trail to collect the money.

Consider this example: If the debtor was a government employee, he would get a pension or an annuity fund, which might be garnishable or lienable. A simple information subpoena to the government agency he works for would yield a *work history.* An information subpoena is a list of questions that courts require the person or entity to answer within fourteen days from the date it is received. If you do not respond to these, you are in contempt of a court order. These court orders can be obtained at the court where the judgment was awarded or they can also be issued by an officer of the court such as an attorney, a marshal, or a sheriff. If you are a party to the lawsuit, you can go into the court and request one. The fee for an information subpoena varies from court to court and county to county. Generally they range from about $15 for a small-claims court subpoena and up to $275 for supreme courts.

Figure out what his area of expertise is. This will tell you which department he works for, and from that you can find the phone number. With your first goal accomplished, you can call him directly. If that doesn't coerce payment, perhaps legal action will.

Hard and Soft Assets Are Fair Game

Tangible assets are those that can be physically touched, like a house or a boat. They are sometimes referred to as hard assets. Intangible assets are assets that can't be physically touched, such as liquid currency, or cash, stocks, bonds, trusts, instruments, other equities and annuities. Assets don't always have a physical spot, and you'll need to look at the total picture of the debtor to find them. All of these external factors will have an impact on defining who this debtor is and which approach would be best to collect what is rightfully yours. Tangible assets are usually more illiquid than intangible assets, meaning that they are harder to liquidate or sell off.

Pretrial Asset Searches Can Be a Valuable Tool

Nonpretrial litigation asset searches can be a way for you to collect money using skip tracing techniques. Some are legal and some are illegal. Pretrial litigation *asset searches* are nonjudicial asset searches. This type of asset search has not been ordered by a court. It is an asset search without court intervention because an index number has not been purchased and the subject was not put on notice. A judicial asset search is one that has been ordered by a court or that was processed through the courts. Judicial and nonjudicial asset searches will maximize the value of distressed assets, while saving money for attorneys, investigators, accountants, creditors, lenders, insurers, receivers, and other professional lots of money. We will discuss these searches at length in chapter 3.

Skip Tracing a Business Debtor Is a Whole Other Ball Game

Skip tracing debtor businesses is also quite common. Some companies are deadbeats. The owners stiff vendors and end-users. Judgments are awarded, but the money can be hard to collect for your clients in some cases. As I said, a different set of laws and statutes applies to searching for the assets of a business, as opposed to searching for the assets of an individual. That means you'll need to employ a different strategy.

If your debtor was a restaurant for example, you could go inside and have dinner and snoop around for important documentation that must be posted. If they have a bar and offer liquor, they will need to have a liquor license. If you can get a peek at that license you will discover the real legal name of the restaurant. It would be hard to start a lawsuit against a business without knowing the true name of the business.

I once had a restaurant debtor-skip and I was having a hard time finding any assets. The restaurant was part of a national franchise chain and was a privately owned corporate store. I did not have the correct legal name to do the search. I went inside and ordered a hamburger platter and a Coke. After I finished eating, I asked for my check. I called over the waitress and told her that I just looked inside my purse and noticed that I forgot my wallet at home with all my identification and all my credit cards. I did have my checkbook with me and I would give her a big tip if she would take my check. She said that they did not take checks, but she would ask the manager. The manager looked angry and then shrugged his shoulders, and she came back and took my check. I told them I would make out the check to "cash" if they wanted, but they said to make it out to the franchise. When the check had cleared my bank the following week, they had endorsed the check with an endorsement stamp. From that I was able to locate the true legal name of the business, the bank account, and the checking account number. I had located all the hidden assets I needed in just one simple step.

One of the reasons corporations and other business-entity types are formed is to protect the owner or the officers and members of the board from personal liability. A common trend now is to get liability insurance for corporate officers so that they are protected from corporate wrongdoing or business mistakes. That would translate into a corporation that is a totally independent entity from the owner or from the officers. A corporation has a FEIN number (federal employer identification number), and an individual has a Social Security number. Corporate liability lies solely on the corporation, and personal liability lies solely on the individual unless the individual signs a personal guarantee. Even with a personal guarantee, it will sometimes be hard to enforce a judgment against a corporation using assets of an individual.

One example of this could be when an individual personally guarantees the debt of a corporation, such as a delinquent phone bill; if the business goes bankrupt and the assets remain in the name of an individual, it might be difficult to enforce that. The reverse will also hold true. When an individual goes bankrupt and forms a corporation and takes over the assets of the individual, that corporation is protected from that liability against the individual.

At Times, Individuals Can Be Held Accountable for the Debts of Their Corporations

In some unusual situations, a corporate entity is used by its owners to perpetuate fraud, circumvent the law, or in some other way accomplish an illegitimate objective. In these cases, the court will ignore the corporate structure by *piercing the corporate veil.*

The following are legal techniques that will allow the courts to pierce the corporate veil and go after the individual for the debts.

1. A party is tricked or misled into dealing with the corporation rather than with the individual.

2. The corporation is set up never to make a profit or always be insolvent, or it is too *thinly capitalized.*

3. The shareholder or director unconditionally guarantees to be personally liable for corporate obligations, corporate debts, or both.

4. Statutory corporate formalities, such as calling required corporation meetings, are not followed.

5. Personal and corporate interests are commingled to the extent that the corporation has no separate identity.

When the corporate privilege is abused for personal benefit and the corporate business is treated in such a careless manner that the corporation and the shareholder in control are no longer separate entities, the court will require an owner to assume personal liability to creditors for the corporation's debts. This is one reason that commercial collections and consumer collections are so different. Because they juggle to see who gets paid and who does not, the collection laws that apply to consumer collections do not apply to commercial collections.

This usually results in negative working capital, which is the state where a company is basically operating with no capital because the company's liabilities exceed the available assets. A company cannot operate with negative working capital for an extended period of time because the company will be unable to meet payment requirements on certain liabilities if the additional funds are not acquired. A company can quickly identify this state by looking at the accounts receivable information and comparing that to accounts payable information. This is also known as being illiquid.

Parent Corporations Are Liable for the Debts of a Newly Acquired Company

When corporations merge or are acquired by other businesses, the successor corporation steps into the shoes of the predecessor corporation and assumes all assets and liabilities of the company. All assets would include, but not be limited to, licenses, vehicles, leases, real property and chattel, bank accounts, inventory and all collateral, all accounts receivable, contracts, all employees, all pensions, all annuities and annuity funds, all trademarks, copyrights and patents, any intellectual property, all furniture, art, advertising rights and other rights, and all equipment.

All liabilities would include all accounts payable, notes payable, debts, obligations, and encumbrances. In a merger or acquisition or sale, all assets and liabilities must be accounted for so that any outstanding debt prior to the sale must be booked at market value or purchase value, so that the debt should still be on the financial statements and owed by the new entity. For example, if ABC Corporation bought out XYZ Corporation, the new business, ABC and XYZ Corporation, will have all the assets transferred to the new balance sheet. Making a motion to amend the judgment would be the next step in satisfaction of that instrument.

Deadbeat Companies Sometimes Go to Great Lengths to Hide Their Correct Legal Name

A case came across my desk recently where the judgment debtors were an individual and a nonoperational corporation. The individual had closed up shop and started up a new corporation with a similar name. He was still the signer on the new account and had closed the old corporate business checking account. The attorney had served a property execution. In some states this is referred to as a writ of execution on the bank. The bank responded that they had no property belonging to the judgment debtor. I explained to the client that the individual was not an account holder just because he was a signer on the account. The account holder is another corporate entity. As an officer of the corporation, the individual has no personal liability. Therefore, it is not property belonging to the individual. It is property belonging to a corporation, separate from the judgment. For the client to collect, he would need to amend the judgment.

Never underestimate the slippery nature of a debtor corporation to hide assets from its creditors. I have seen cases where the debtor has his business in New York and has their bank account in New Jersey. Because New York judgments can only be enforced in New York, you will need to get a new judgment in New Jersey or certify and file it in New Jersey. This can be a costly and time-consuming endeavor for many. Sometimes it is easier to get an out-of-state attorney to do the paper pushing for you. Precise information can sometimes be the difference between collecting a judgment or getting nothing.

Some of these corporations are extremely deceptive; they have been known to operate with two different names or very similar names located at the same address. I have seen DEF Consortium for its business name, but the company maintained accounts for DEF Holdings and DEF Management. I have also seen where a corporation uses the owner's Social Security number instead of its federal employer identification number.

Make sure to verify the true legal name of the corporation, because in some instances, debtors try to camouflage their real correct legal identity in order to evade creditors. This is only because the corporation is the skip. If it was a person, it would be different. They also use variations of words like LTD, LLC, LP, and Inc so that the name on the certificate of incorporation does not match the real name of the debtor corporation. Some of these corporate debtors also set up accounts for business trusts. The best way to settle a case is to be ready for a settlement.

It is also vital to know which reference sources to use in which situations and to know which sources are available to you. For example, if you are skip tracing a person, you would not go the Secretary of State website or to the Securities and Exchange Commission's website to research unless the person is self-employed, and you are investigating his company. Many Secretary of State websites do not allow you to search for a principal or for officers, but some states do. This is exactly why deciding when to use a subscription database or a public one is helpful. Always go to the source when it is available. The source in this case is free, and it is the Secretary of State. They have the custodial responsibility of holding corporate records in their respective states.

If the business you are researching is a publicly traded corporation, then the SEC requires it to file registration statements, periodic reports, and other forms electronically through Edgar. Edgar means the Electronic Data-Gathering, Analysis, and Retrieval system. Anyone can access and download this information for free, and it is the source. If your search does not yield results, that is the time to go to a fee-based database like D&B or the Better Business Bureau. Sometimes records fall through the cracks and are not listed with the Secretary of States until future dates, but they are picked up by the private companies that use private public record researchers, in some cases. That is one reason why sometimes you get a hit in one database, and it will be a no-hit in another database; at other times, it is an oversight.

Tracking down deadbeat individuals and corporations will very likely represent (or already does represent) a big part of your business. The trick is to find the hidden assets, and then take all legal means to collect on the debt. But what happens when the person you're looking for is actually a stolen identity? A phantom? Yes, there's a thief behind that fake identity, and there's most often a real person (a victim) behind that fake identity as well. But what assets can you collect? None, except if you get them from the thief. Let's take a hard look at the issue of identity theft as a whole, and as it relates to skip tracing.

The Debt May Be Real, but in Cases of Identity Theft, There Are No Assets to Collect

Many times I was given a case to work and only after going through several steps did I realize that the debtor I thought I was looking for was actually a victim of identity theft and a false record had been created. There was no possibility whatsoever that this debt would ever be collected because it was a debt made by a fictitious person. The skip tracer needs to understand this fact and not waste any time. A general rule of thumb when doing the basic intelligence gathering in a case is to establish that the subject is a real person.

As of 2012, America's fastest growing crime continues to be fraud and identity theft. According to the FTC reference center, it is an $18 billion industry with feeding industries adding to the real cost. Based on a range of information gathered from public and private resources, this figure exceeds $50 billion. That figure does not include phishing, spoofing, skimming, hijacking, forging, pharming, and other electronic frauds. How these crimes happen and how to avoid them is still baffling our world; with globalization taking hold, it becomes more difficult to control other countries' dos and don'ts. But, depending on the crime, the meat and potatoes of the crime occurs at the local level.

Thieves Have Many Clever Ways to Steal a Person's Identity

Here are a few of the common ways thieves rob victims of information that can be used to create fake identities and perpetrate fraud.

Phishing: This is a way of attempting to acquire information such as usernames, passwords, and credit card details by masquerading as a trustworthy entity in an electronic communication. *Spear phishing* attempts are directed at specific individuals or companies. Attackers may gather personal information about their target to increase their probability of success. *Clone phishing* is a type of phishing attack whereby a legitimate, and previously delivered, e-mail containing an attachment or link has had its content and recipient addresses taken and used to create an almost identical or cloned email. The attachment or link within the e-mail is replaced with a malicious version and then sent from an e-mail address spoofed to appear to come from the original sender. It may claim to be a resend of the original or an updated version to the original.

Spoofing: This is e-mail activity in which the sender address and other parts of the e-mail header are altered to appear as though the e-mail originated from a different source. Because core protocol doesn't provide any authentication, it is easy to impersonate and forge e-mails. *Caller ID spoofing* makes caller ID information now next to useless. Spoofing technology enables someone to make it seem as though they are calling from your telephone when they are not. The use of this technology for deceptive purposes is illegal.

Skimming: This is a slang term that refers to taking cash off the top. Skimming may additionally be the direct theft of the cash the perpetrator hides when stealing from an employer, business partners, or anyone or anything. *Credit card skimming* is theft of credit card information used in an otherwise legitimate transaction. For example, you might go to a restaurant and give your card to the waiter to charge your bill, and then they skim (copy) the information off your card and use it to create a new card; the card security code would be jotted down manually. More sophisticated types have come up with a small electronic device called a skimmer to swipe and store hundreds of victims' credit card numbers in high volume stores.

Hijacking: This term applies to stealing something while it is in progress. It usually refers to an airplane or ship being hijacked, but it also refers to home page hijacking, meaning it takes you to a place that is make-believe. One example of this is when you get an e-mail supposedly from your bank, and it says to "click here" to log in to your account. When you click on that link, it takes you to a website that was created just to steal your personal information. Many spyware programs display advertisements. Some programs simply display pop-up ads. Spyware operators present this feature as desirable to advertisers, who may buy ad placement in pop-ups displayed when the user visits a particular site. It is also one of the purposes for which spyware programs gather information on user behavior. There is also spyware protection available to remove them. Be careful of computer insecurity.

Forging: Forging a counterfeit credit card can be done easily and cheaply once you have all the information you need. In the context of network security, forging is a situation in which one person or program successfully masquerades as another by falsifying data and then gaining an illegitimate advantage.

Pharming: This is a hacker's attack intended to redirect a website's traffic to another, bogus site. *Pharming* is a new term based on the words *farming* and *phishing*. In recent years, both pharming and phishing have been used to gain information for online identity theft.

Here's a sample of the other ways identity thieves commit their crimes:Scammers file a change-of-address form in someone else's name to divert mail and gather personal and financial data.

- Thieves steal credit card payments and other outgoing mail from private curbside mailboxes.

- Perpetrators (perps) lift driver's license numbers, Social Security numbers, phone numbers, or other identifiers from checks.

- Perps steal mail, especially envelopes containing bill payments, from unlocked, unguarded out-boxes at work.

- Crooks go Dumpster diving by digging through garbage cans or community Dumpsters in search of canceled checks, credit card and bank statements, or preapproved credit card offers.

- Criminals steal discarded applications for preapproved credit cards and fill them out with a different address.

- Robbers steal wallets and purses—and all of the credit and identification cards inside them.

- Con artists take important documents such as birth certificates, passports, copies of tax returns, Social Security cards, and the like during a burglary of your house. They steal the Social Security numbers and identities of children, who are especially vulnerable because they don't have credit histories, and it may be many years before the theft is discovered.

- Fraudsters lift names and Social Security numbers from such documents as a driver's license, employee badge, student ID card, check, or medical chart.

- Bandits use personal information from a who's who book or a newspaper article.

- Thugs use the personal information of a relative or someone he or she knows well, perhaps by being a frequent visitor to their home.

- Prowlers pretend to be government officials or legitimate businesspeople who need to gather personal information from credit reporting agencies or other sources.

- Safecrackers hack into a computer that contains your personal records and steal the data.

- Burglars buy records stolen by a fellow employee who's been bribed.

- Pilferers "shoulder surf" by watching from a nearby location as he or she punches in a telephone calling card number or by listening in on a conversation in which the victim provides a credit card number over the telephone in a public place.

- Peepers use the camera in a cell phone to photograph someone's credit card or ATM card while he or she is using an ATM machine or buying something in a store.

- Housebreakers phish by sending a legitimate-looking e-mail that directs you to a phony website that looks legitimate and asks for your personal and financial data.

- Hackers *pharm*, which means criminals hijack whole domains to their own sites and gather the personal and financial data of users who believe they're communicating through their customary service provider.

- Crackers send fraudulent spam e-mails that promise huge prizes or bargains in return for personal and financial information.

- Cheats skim by having a dishonest merchant secretly copy the magnetic strip on the back of your credit or debit card in order to make a counterfeit card that can then be sold.

- Swindlers send a fake electronic IRS form to gather personal information and financial data. (Note: The IRS never requests information by e-mail.)

These creeps will go into stores and apply for credit using a make-believe driver's license and a false identity. Some stores will even issue a temporary card right on the spot if the credit application is approved. That means the sneaks can shop on the spot for a set value. The address on the application is different from the address on the driver's license, and that is why the victim does not know he has been victimized. The perp is off with the goods, and the store is left holding the bag and looking for the criminal. In some cases, they actually have the goods shipped to another address. They start to transpose numbers in the Social Security number and are off to multiple identities to buy goods for personal use or to sell them. The victim doesn't even find out he has been compromised for many months—maybe up to three months—at which time the account will go into collection status, and skip tracers try to figure it out. They might even contact you to find out what happened, in which case, it is too late. The fraud has already been committed.

If a Client Is the Victim of Identity Theft, Certain Steps Need to Be Taken Immediately

Obviously, if one of your clients is a victim of identity theft, you need to have them file a police report where they live and also file a police report in the county where the crime was committed. They will need to advise all three credit bureaus and have a fraud alert put on their report. They will need to add a *consumer statement* to their credit report asking that no one issue credit without contacting them first. They should contact the Federal Trade Commission; the FTC has other resources and it monitors these crimes. They should get a privacy protection agency to monitor their credit report for suspicious activity and any new inquiries or new lines of credit being extended. These agencies are worth the price.

Privacy laws protect who has access to what information. Although a national identification card may not be the solution to the problem, one safe bet is for the store or issuer to be able to verify if the one item being used as the valid piece of identification *is* a valid license and if it *was issued* by the Department of Motor Vehicles or the real regulatory authority. This could be done at the same time they are running the credit report. It seems this would stop or deter the crime significantly. Other forms of biometrics, such as thumbprint signatures and other digital signatures that appear to be hacker proof seem to all be flawed in some way and can be cracked, so other methods are advised. Research-and-development companies within security companies keep trying to patent new properties. Children and the deceased are also used to perpetrate this crime. Social behaviors put consumers at risk and smart-phone owners experience a greater incidence of fraud. Data breaches are increasing and more damaging.

Here is a pie chart showing the different types of fraud from federal statistics for 2012.

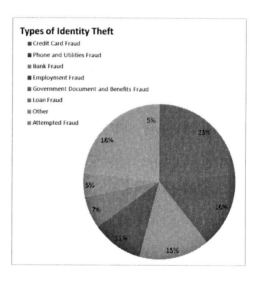

Types of Identity Theft
- Credit Card Fraud
- Phone and Utilities Fraud
- Bank Fraud
- Employment Fraud
- Government Document and Benefits Fraud
- Loan Fraud
- Other
- Attempted Fraud

So, clearly identity theft will play a part in your business. Chances are you will encounter it when you're out looking for a debtor. When you do, you'll probably be on the hook for all the time you spent on the case, and you won't get paid. Write it off as the cost of doing business. You can avoid some of the losses by verifying right away that the subject you seek is real and that there are assets to collect. That's just good business sense!

> *Many receive advice, but only the wise profit from it.*
>
> —*Publilius Syrus*

Chapter 3
Collecting the Debts

He went broke slowly and then all at once.

—Ernest Hemingway

It's a fact that you or your client can win a judgment against a debtor if nonpayment of the debt can be proven, but it is also a fact that judgments don't mean the debtor will actually pay up. When seeking and collecting a judgment, skip tracers act like the support staff of the attorney of record and the client. As I've said, there are different types of assets, and there are different types of asset searches, but the overall goal is to collect what is owed. Below are a number of tools for finding hidden assets and collecting debts.

Asset Searches Are a Routine Part of Skip Tracing, Especially before a Trial

Pretrial asset searches: These are usually requested when the attorney-client needs to determine the ability of the subject to pay. This is not the only reason, but it is the most popular. Other reasons for these requests are to determine if the attorney wants to invest time and effort to sue in the case or he wants to know if there will be money to award if the lawsuit is won. Other times, the client will want to decide if the subject of the investigation is just simply credit worthy. They might need this information to determine if they want to become involved in any kind of partnership with the subject. These types of arrangements in business become similar to marriages because they can lead to divorce. In matrimonial cases, the spouses want to determine before getting divorced what assets might be hidden or undisclosed by the other spouse.

Pretrial litigation asset searches conducted on businesses should not be confused with the same type of asset search for individuals. After the Gramm–Leach–Bliley Act (GLB) became law over a decade ago, the methods for gathering of information changed from black to white. There were no longer any shades of gray allowed. The GLB did not make asset searches illegal—it changed the way we perform asset searches on consumers, but not on corporate debtors.

If the search relates to a consumer credit transaction, then it is governed by the Fair Credit Reporting Act (FCRA). We'll discuss FCRA in the next chapter. Businesses cannot be involved in consumer credit transactions because they are a business. A whole different set of laws govern that area, mainly the Uniform Commercial Code (UCC). While the basics of the asset search will be similar, in the actual execution, they will be different. They cannot be compared.

Pretrial litigation asset searches for both individuals and businesses (including nonprofits) have many similarities. The Freedom of Information Act (FOIA) has made public records open to search requests. Publically available information is searchable for both financial and nonfinancial information. All leave paper trails that can be followed if we look beyond the basics and follow the laws. Look beyond the transaction.

Many traditional legal methods are not available for pretrial litigation asset searches because there is no permissible purpose to conduct the search. Other methods are available for litigation support and recoveries.

Nonjudicial asset search: This is an asset search that has not been ordered by a court and is without court intervention. When a loan default occurs, the homeowner or borrower will be mailed a default letter, and in many states, a *notice of default* will be recorded at approximately the same time. If the homeowner does not cure the default, a *notice of sale* will be mailed to the homeowner, posted in public places, recorded at the county recorder's office, and published in area legal publications. That will create a public record. After the legally required time period has expired, a public auction will be held, with the highest bidder becoming the owner of the property. Title is distinct from possession, a right that often accompanies ownership but is not sufficient to prove it. Nonjudicial asset searches give us the power to foreclose on a property without court approval.

Judicial asset search: This is an asset search that has been ordered by a court or that is processed through the courts. The first step is the lender files a complaint and a recording a notice of *lis pendens*. *Lis pendens* is Latin for "suit pending" and simply means written notice that a lawsuit has been filed which concerns the title to real property or some interest. The *complaint* will state what the debt is, and why the default should allow the lender to foreclose and take the property given as security for the loan.

The homeowner will be served notice of the complaint, either by mailing, direct service, or publication of the notice, and will have the opportunity to be heard before the court. If the court finds the debt valid, and in default, it will issue a judgment for the total amount owed, including the costs of the foreclosure process.

After the judgment has been entered, a writ will be issued by the court authorizing a sheriff's sale. The *sheriff's sale* is an auction, open to anyone, and is held in a public place, which can range from in front of the courthouse steps, to in front of the property being auctioned. We will discuss this later. Sheriff's sales will require either cash to be paid at the time of sale, or a substantial deposit, with the balance paid later. Check your local procedures carefully. At the end of the auction, the highest bidder will be the owner of the property, subject to the court's confirmation of the sale.

After the court has confirmed the sale, a sheriff's deed will be prepared and delivered to the highest bidder. When that deed is recorded, the highest bidder is the owner of the property. After the court has confirmed the sale, a sheriff's deed will be prepared and delivered to the highest bidder; when that deed is recorded, the highest bidder is the owner of the property. Title is distinct from possession, a right that often accompanies ownership but is not sufficient to prove it. Sometimes, both possession and title may be transferred independently of each other.

The Real Estate Industry Is a Hot Prospect for New Skip Tracers

If your skip is in the real estate industry for example, you will need to search in an industry that is specific to that and them. If your skip is a doctor, the same logic holds true. The real estate industry was very heavily damaged in large part due to criminals who specifically targeted them. The real estate industry has a large volume of work for skip tracers because they have been victims of so many scams and frauds.

I had worked on a case not long ago where my client was a victim of real estate fraud. She had inherited a two-family house in Brooklyn, New York, when her father passed away. She had moved to the house and taken possession of it, but had not received the deed yet. They had a tenant living on the second floor who apparently had the father sign the title over to them for a refinance deal—that was the fraud. This client was in court trying to prove that the house was now hers and trying to get the tenant evicted. As this book goes to press, she was still in court proceedings. She was waiting for an order to have the marshal go in to evict the tenant.

If a borrower faces some kind of economic hardship or downturn and the borrower's loan goes into default, the lender then has to decide what to do. Is a negotiated solution the best answer? Or should the lender commence proceedings? The answer is never an easy one for the lender. There are numerous practical, economic, and legal factors to consider, and they may not all point to the same solution. Judicial and nonjudicial asset searches will maximize the value of distressed assets and inventory while saving creditors, lenders, insurers, lawyers, receivers, and other financial professionals lots of money. The new federal agency *Consumer Protection Bureau* (CPB) regulates most activity in this area for now. Credit is a privilege and not a right. We earn it. Manage it wisely, and you'll have great assets.

One of the Most Powerful Weapons in the Skip Tracing Arsenal Is the Judgment Debtor Exam

Judgment debtor exam: This is a preferred tool of the attorney and the skip tracer. If the judgment isn't paid, the judgment creditor may get an *order for examination of judgment debtor*. This is also known as the judgment debtor exam or OEX. This is a procedure used to find out where the judgment debtor works, keeps money, and what assets he or she possesses.

Obtaining the judgment is easy. Collecting the judgment is the challenging task. So, how do you proceed to collect the judgment? You can contact the judgment debtor by letter, stating the amount owed, judgment date, the legal debt, and that you expect payment in full. Have them contact you and state that this letter gives them the opportunity to work out a payment arrangement amicably, before involuntary collection actions occur. You worked so hard to obtain your judgment; now comes the hard part. What do you do with it?

The exam is held to question the debtor about their ability to pay the debt owed to you or your client. You may approach the judgment debtor as though you are trying to assist in finding a solution to their debts. This is a fact-finding mission. You may ask about their current employer, the location of their bank accounts, personal assets, automobiles registered in their name, life insurance, and even the amount of cash on hand. You can then ask the judge to order the debtor to turn over those assets. All the information gathered may assist you in the immediate collection of your judgment in the event a payment plan cannot be adhered to by the debtor. Your other options to plan out your strategy will be discussed further.

As we just discussed, the party to a lawsuit who owes money is also known as a judgment debtor. The *order for examination* will be served on the debtor along with a subpoena to appear in court and often is accompanied with a request to bring documents related to wages, banks accounts, and other holdings. The judgment debtor must appear in court to answer questions by the creditor's lawyer. The judgment debtor must comply with the order by appearing in court or a warrant will be issued for their arrest.

Different courts call this a *supplemental examination, debtor examination, interrogatories,* or *disclosure hearing.* We will discuss this further in our next topic. You will need to fill out paperwork with the court for an order to start this procedure if it is your judgment. If the judgment is for a client, the attorney usually handles the process. Some useful information to get from the judgment debtor during the procedure would include a description of any real estate owned; spouse's name and employment; Social Security numbers; driver's license number; bank locations and account numbers; current employment and the employer name and address, when and how often paid, and salary amount. Other income types such as commissions, rental income, part-time employment, royalties, interest, etc. are also part of the exam. You can also question the debtor regarding property, such as stock, interest in a business, type and location of vehicles owned, etc. It's a good idea to round out the questioning with a general question such as, "Do you have any property, personal effects, cash, or other assets that you haven't yet mentioned? If so, explain."

Service of process: This is the procedure employed to give legal notice to a person, such as a defendant, of a court or administrative body's exercise of its jurisdiction over that person so as to enable that person to respond to the proceeding before the court, body, or other tribunal. Usually, notice is furnished by delivering a set of court documents called *process* to the person to be served. Each jurisdiction has rules regarding the means of service of process. Most states allow substituted service in almost all lawsuits unless you are serving a corporation, limited liability corporation (LLC), limited liability partnership (LLP), professional corporation

(PC), or other business entity; in those cases, personal service must be achieved by serving the documents to the registered agent of a business entity. When a party to be served is unavailable for personal service, many jurisdictions allow for substituted service.

Substituted service allows the process server to leave service documents with another responsible individual such as cohabiting adults. Service by mail is permitted by most US jurisdictions. Mail is permitted in New York State. For service on defendants located in other US states or foreign countries, check local procedures. Service on a defendant who resides in a state or country outside the jurisdiction of the court must comply with special procedures.

A Neat Trick during a Debtor Exam Is to Ask to See the Person's Key Chain

When you conduct your OEX, start your examination by setting the ground rules with your debtor. Look your debtor in the eye and say, "Hello. We'll start by you completing this questionnaire. When you are done, I'll ask you some questions about your assets. While answering the questionnaire and my follow-up questions, be as thorough as possible. Do you have any questions before we begin?" You control the examination. Do not allow your debtor to run over you.

Take a look at your debtor's key chain. Ask your debtor to show you his or her keys, and then ask what each key goes to. If it is a car, ask the make, model, year, and who owns it. If one of the keys goes to a house or a commercial building, ask who the owner is and where it is located. If the debtor denies ownership of the item for which he or she has a key, then ask why he or she has a key to something he or she does not own. Does it belong to the debtor's employer? Who is his or her employer? You do not want to dive right in and ask your debtor, "Where do you bank?" Your debtor will understand the significance of this question and run right out after the examination hearing to close accounts. Bury the question about your debtor's bank account information in the middle of other questions. Make the question about his or her bank account seem insignificant so that you do not draw attention to the issue.

If you do find out about a bank account, then *immediately after completing your debtor's examination, go get a restraining order to prevent the debtor from hightailing it out of town with the loot.* If the debtor refuses to answer a question, the lawyer may seek an order from the judge, compelling the debtor to answer the question. Clearly ask your debtor if each asset mentioned or identified in the questionnaire is owned or leased. If your debtor says that a particular asset is owned but not paid off, then follow up and find out how much, if any, is still owed on it, and to whom. The business employee or owner may try to stonewall you or act aloof, but do not let it last long. Equity demands that the law strike a balance between the right of the creditor to collect and the right of the debtor to due process.

If the examinee has any interests in general or limited partnerships (including limited liability partnerships and possibly limited liability companies operating as partnerships), you must prepare and obtain a charging order, which will give the creditor the right to receive distributions until the obligation is satisfied. Again, if the judgment is yours, you can file the paperwork, though you'll probably want your lawyer to do it. If the judgment involved is your client's, the representing attorney will handle the process. Turnover orders can require the immediate surrender to the creditor, or to the court, of an asset under the control of an examinee. You must seek a turnover order from the judge before concluding the exam and dismissing the debtor or risk giving the debtor an opportunity to dispose of the asset.

Once You Get the Judgment, It's Up to You and the Attorney to Go after the Money, and That Can Be Challenging

Postjudgment collection strategies: These are very extensive and have many resources. A judgment lien on real property is the one of the most used tools. A *lien* is a financial claim you hold against someone else's real property as a result of a judgment awarded in your favor or in favor of your client. Because of your claim or your client's claim, the owner of this property cannot sell or transfer title to the property to anyone else until your financial claim is satisfied. A judgment lien can be enforced by forcing foreclosure on the real property against which you levied the lien. Learning how to file a lien online will save you a lot of time and, at the same time, prevent some of the mistakes that could invalidate your claim. Courts across the country have modernized the way they do business, and it is not unusual to have a lot of the procedures take place online. E-filing is the way of the future.

The judgment lien is satisfied from the sale proceeds when the debtor sells the real property. In the meantime, the creditor has a lien against the property. In effect this secures payment of the judgment, and the outstanding balance of the judgment increases due to the addition of statutory interest on the amount. If the debtor should move or if the debtor owns real property in another county, the creditor may obtain a transcript of judgment from the county clerk's office and file it in another county. Once a transcript is filed with the county clerk, there is a public record of the judgment against the debtor which could affect the debtor's credit rating or ability to borrow money. A judgment against the debtor remains as a lien against real property for a period of ten years, renewable for an additional ten years in New York. Every state has different rules for sunsetting debt.

Filing a Lien against a Debtor's Personal Property Is an Effective Way to Up the Odds That Your Client Will Get Paid—Eventually

Personal property liens: These are another widely used resource. To create a judgment lien against personal property, the judgment creditor typically files a notice of judgment lien with the Secretary of State where the judgment debtor resides. The judgment lien notice contains information about the judgment creditor, the judgment debtor, the date, court of issuance and amount of the judgment, and the date that a copy the notice was sent to the judgment debtor.

A judgment lien against personal property of the judgment debtor is typically effective against property upon which a security interest may be perfected, such as accounts receivable, chattel paper, equipment, farm products, and negotiable documents of title. Some states exclude certain property such as motor vehicles and inventory of a retail merchant held for sale. As with a real property lien, typically the judgment is satisfied from the sale proceeds when the judgment debtor sells property that is subject to the lien.

Generally speaking, any property of the judgment debtor which is transferred without satisfaction of the judgment is transferred subject to the lien. This means that if the lien is not satisfied prior to the transfer being made, the property remains subject to the lien in the hands of the transferee. The levy on, or seizure of, a judgment debtor's personal property by the use of a property execution is the most common method for enforcing a money judgment. When navigating the minefield of judgment liens versus security interests, take special care of the priority interests that will arise.

It can really pay big dividends in time and money if skip tracers learn the law, or if they team up with attorneys in a mutually beneficial relationship.

Security interest: This is a property interest created by agreement or by operation of law over assets to secure the performance of an obligation, usually the payment of a debt. It gives the beneficiary of the security interest certain preferential rights in the disposition of secured assets. Such rights vary according to the type of security interest, but in most cases, a holder of the security interest is entitled to seize, and usually sell, the property to discharge the debt that the security interest secures.

Legal lien: In most common law systems, a legal lien is a right to retain physical possession of tangible assets as security for the underlying obligations. It is a form of security, and possession of the assets must be transferred to and maintained by the secured party. The right is purely passive; the secured party has no right to sell the assets—merely a right to refuse to return them until paid. Priority between a judgment lien on personal property and a conflicting security interest in the same personal property shall be determined according to priority in time of filing or perfection.

Judgment lien: This type of lien is a subordinate to a security interest which is prior and perfected. A secured party who advances additional monies, based on their security interest, would be *ahead* in priority over a perfected judgment lien. The secured party is fully secured as to all future advances based on their *security agreement* and the perfected UCC, as long as the secured party has not received a notice of judgment lien. After the secured lender has physically received the notice of judgment lien, the secured party will be fully secured ahead of all judgment creditors for all advances made before the judgment lien.

Priorities and liens on real property is another basic tool for docketing the judgment. No transfer of an interest of the judgment debtor in real property, against which property a money judgment may be enforced, is effective against the judgment creditor. Either from the time of the docketing of the judgment with the clerk of the county in which the property is located until ten years after filing of the judgment-roll, or from the time of the filing with such clerk of a notice of levy pursuant to an execution until the execution is returned, except:

- A transfer or the payment of the proceeds of a judicial sale, which shall include an execution sale, in satisfaction either of a judgment or of a judgment where a notice of levy pursuant to an execution was previously so filed.

- A transfer in satisfaction of a mortgage given to secure the payment of the purchase price of the judgment debtor's interest in the property.

- A transfer to a purchaser for value at a judicial sale, which shall include an execution sale.

- When the judgment was entered after the death of the judgment debtor.

- When the judgment debtor is the state, an officer, department, board or commission of the state, or a municipal corporation.

- When the judgment debtor is the personal representative of a decedent and the judgment was awarded in an action against him in his representative capacity.

Extension of lien: When time expires on a lien, the most common method is to file an extension. Upon motion of the judgment creditor, upon notice to the judgment debtor, served personally or by registered or certified mail, return receipt requested, to the last known address of the judgment debtor, the court may order that the lien of a money judgment upon real property be effective after the expiration of ten years from the filing of the judgment-roll, for a period no longer than the time during which the judgment creditor was stayed from enforcing the judgment. Or the time necessary to complete advertisement and sale of real property pursuant to an execution delivered to a sheriff prior to the expiration of ten years from the filing of the judgment. Different states have different time periods and rules and statutes.

The procedures and creditor priority outlines the rules when the sheriff sells off property. The sheriff seizes or levies upon property for the purpose of satisfying a judgment. This is done by liquidating the assets, by converting the asset into cash. This is done by holding a *sheriff's sale* which is a *public auction*. The process starts with advertisements in the local county newspapers and other media to notify the public of the impending sheriff's auction and to provide the address of the property, auction date, place, and other relevant information. At the time of the auction, interested buyers are asked to bid on the property being auctioned, and the highest bidder wins the right to buy it. Sheriff's sales are public auctions, so anyone can bid. These vary from county to county and state to state.

Let the Buyer Beware at Public Auctions

There are a number of disadvantages to consider prior to bidding at any sheriff's sale. A buyer has to conduct his or her own title search and confirm details on the real estate being considered prior to bidding at the public auction. This can very well represent lost time and money if the buyer does not win the bid. A buyer will in most cases have to buy a property being auctioned without prior inspection and in *as is* condition. If a property happens to be occupied by a tenant or previous owner, it is the responsibility of a buyer to remove the occupant. Security interests of secured creditors get liquidated first in order of priority. Vehicle auction sales are usually conducted by the marshal in New York City, but the sheriff in other counties and the constables in still other counties. So the procedures will vary from state to state and county to county.

The order in which creditors are paid when the assets of a borrower are liquidated are very simply—first to file! *Creditor priority* is established under the first-to-file rule in the Uniform Commercial Code. The UCC was first published in 1952 and is a body of laws governing commercial transactions. The code is designed for interstate transactions, but really applies to all aspects of business law. UCC is not federal law, but every state has adopted the code and modified it to meet its individual needs. It then becomes state law. It governs all aspects of business dealings and is meant to further uniformity and fair dealing in business and commercial transactions.

Getting your client at the head of the line of creditors by filing first will bolster the odds of settling some or part of the debt.

One very simple and basic example to use would be when a company buys a piece of equipment to make something, such as an oven to bake cakes. Then the bakery cannot make the payments on the oven because it is not doing well and doesn't have the money. The UCC would dictate legal process to take. In the case of the oven, the oven manufacturer would have made a UCC filing in the bakery's state. If the bakery can't make the payments, then the oven manufacturer has the right to take back the oven. If they don't give back the oven, then the manufacturer has the right to have the sheriff come in and auction off the oven so that the manufacturer can be made whole again. Many debtors would like the oven manufacturer to go away and just give them the oven because they need it, but that would not be fair to the manufacturer. The UCC covers all kinds of very complicated transactions. This example is just to give you an idea of how the methodology behind the law works. Here is a summary as it applies to creditor priority: creditors holding a security interest in collateral are paid before unsecured creditors. As a general rule, holders of secured claims are paid in the order their claims were filed, starting with the earliest recorded lien. Whoever gets the claim perfected first is the first-priority creditor—so it's a race to be the first to file.

Income executions: Income executions (also called *wage garnishments*) and other property levies are ways to generate residual income. Many think of these property executions as multiple streams of income, and entrepreneurs look forward to these repeat payments. In addition to a lien on personal property, a creditor may also use other enforcement methods to collect a debt. The creditor can file an income execution or wage garnishment to obtain a percentage of the debtor's earnings to apply to the judgment. The judgment creditor or the lawyer may contact the agents of the court for the procedure to file an income execution.

Again, as with the procedure for seizing personal property, the creditor will need to inform the marshal, sheriff, or the constable about certain information, namely, the debtor's employer, the employer's address and wages of the debtor, and the Social Security number. This information can be obtained by requesting an information subpoena from the city court clerk. Additionally, a transcript of judgment must be filed with the county clerk before the marshal or the sheriff will proceed to enforce a judgment by income execution.

Some Debtors File for Bankruptcy instead of Paying Up

If a debtor files for bankruptcy during the collection proceedings, then all further collection efforts cease until the debtor is released from bankruptcy court. The creditor should contact the trustee in bankruptcy to determine if the debt will be paid or discharged by the bankruptcy court.

Assignment orders: Any person or corporation may file an assignment of judgment. The assignee is entitled to the use of the court's services for the purpose of collection, and may purchase information subpoenas, exemplifications, certifications, transcript of judgments, etc. When an assignment is filed, court records of both the docket card and the electronic record must be updated with the name and address of the assignee, who becomes the judgment creditor from that point on.

Deficiency action: This is one in which the secured creditor, having repossessed collateral securing the obligation, seeks a judgment for the unpaid balance from the debtor and any guarantors. Is it worth it to a lesser to pursue a deficiency action, after making sure it has complied with the UCC? Careful legal analysis and sound business judgment should lead the way for the creditor's rights. Deficiency actions are brought pursuant to state laws adopted from the Uniform Commercial Code (UCC), and the intricacies of deficiency claims need to be scrutinized under pertinent sections. These actions vary and are not always granted based on deficiency judgments. They can also result from other types of transactions, like leases or other commercial contracts and other types of paper.

In the state of New York, plaintiffs may file for *deficiency judgments* from defendants in the event that a foreclosure sale failed to compensate for the outstanding original loan obligations. The deficiency is the difference between the sum due the lender, the debt as assessed in the judgment of foreclosure and sale, and the greater of the amount bid at the foreclosure sale or the value of the property on the date of the sale.

Debtors Have Plenty of Rights, and Many Assets Are Exempt from Judgments

Debtor exemptions: These also vary from state to state. In New York, personal property exempt from application to the satisfaction of money judgments includes a wide range of items at various values. Some of these are as follows:

- food for sixty days

- stoves with fuel for sixty days; one refrigerator

- crockery, tableware, and cooking utensils necessary for the judgment debtor and his/her family

- family Bibles, pictures, schoolbooks and other books not exceeding $50 in total value

- seats in houses of worship

- pets and animal food for sixty days having a value no greater than $400

- all clothing and household furniture

- one radio receiver and one television

- a wedding ring and a watch not exceeding $35 in total value

- necessary tools, implements, farm machinery, professional instruments, furniture and library related to judgment debtor's profession or calling, not exceeding $600 in value

- property of another held in trust for the judgment debtor, including the judgment debtor's interest in a retirement plan

- 90 percent of income or other payments by such a trust other than retirement plan

- 90 percent of current earnings for the judgment debtor's personal services

- payments made for support of a spouse or child

- medical or dental accessories to the human body; life-sustaining equipment; and a guide, service, or hearing dog, together with its food, unless such items are determined to be unnecessary for the reasonable requirements of the judgment debtor or his/her dependents

- military pay and benefits

- any form of public assistance

- 90 percent of money due for payment for the sale of milk produced on the judgment debtor's farm and delivered for his/her account to a licensed milk dealer

- security deposits for the rental of residential real estate or for utility services

- the loan or surrender value of the judgment debtor's life insurance policy

- certain funds maintained in a college choice tuition savings program trust fund

- up to $10,000 of equity in residential real property, the shares of a cooperative apartment corporation, a condominium unit, or a mobile home

- a family or private cemetery not greater than one-fourth of an acre in size

Exempt Income Protection Act: This amends Article 52 of the New York Civil Practice Law and Rules (CPLR) and limits the ability of judgment creditors and others to restrain Social Security income and other exempt funds in relation to restraint, execution, income execution, and levy procedures with the purpose of establishing a procedure for the execution of money judgments on bank accounts consistent with the aims of state and federal laws exempting certain income from debt collection. Under EIPA, bank accounts cannot be frozen if the balance is less than $2,625 if the account contains directly deposited exempt benefits, including Social Security, SSI, veterans benefits, disability, pensions, child support, spousal maintenance, workers compensation, unemployment insurance, public assistance, railroad retirement benefits, and black lung benefits. Effective April 1, 2012, the amount of the exemption was increased to $2,625, and as such, financial institutions will not restrain an account that has less than this amount. Only monies in excess of $2,625 can be frozen to satisfy a judgment. For example, if you restrained an account that had $5,000 on deposit, only $2,375 may be available. The remainder would be exempt.

Property executions: Serving a bank a property execution is a big gamble. A gamble is an enterprise undertaken or attempted with a risk of loss and a chance of profit or success. It is characterized by a balance between winning and losing that is governed by a mixture of skill and chance. While we want an opportunity to obtain a benefit from indulging, sometimes we come in last, and there is nothing left for us. That is not always true.

Beyond the basics, the balance in a bank account changes from moment to moment, because account balances vary or fluctuate and change from minute to minute depending on what items are presented for payment or which debits are paid out. Some banks will not verify funds on an account for that reason. For example, you verify that a $50 check will clear the account and simultaneously an ACH debit is being processed against the same account. Now the bank has claimed that your check can be paid, but there are not enough funds

in the account to clear both checks. So what
balance in that account is at that moment cann
be determined because funds that are in the a
may not be available for accessing yet because iney
have not cleared the processing process.

Serving a bank is therefore a very big gamble.
Technically, funds should be available, but because
of time constraints, these can be quite complicated to
calculate. This is why the rule of first come, first served
is so appropriate to use in this example. Handling costs
must also be considered, because even in this cyber
age of electronic processing, maintenance becomes
an integral part of the process and another variable for
consideration. Transaction costs play another important
role in the liquid balance. All these factors that are
intangible in scope have tangible effects on the running
balance and are calculated at midnight, in most cases
(especially as they apply to recurring fees or charges). But
many institutions run a dynamic balance that changes
from second to second.

Fraudster Intentional Skips Are the Worst Kind to Run Across When Trying to Collect Debts, but Even the Hard-Core Fraudster Can Be Brought to Justice

I sometimes have clients who need to have an account
monitored because they want to serve it, and it is the only
account the debtor has. I have seen career debtors who
keep a $5 balance in a bank account. They get paid
every Friday and the funds go into the direct deposit
account, but by the time Monday morning rolls around,

there is no balance left in the account. They disbursed all the funds to pay bills and debit what they wanted. Many of these are hard-core intentional skips who have, in many instances, premeditated the debt and devised a way to avoid repayment. Whatever method of operation they have devised, there is almost never a simple way to crack it.

Timing is everything, but unforeseen circumstances can put a damper on any plan. While it is important to have a strategy, make sure to leave room for the latest unexpected disaster. Individual attorney firms are seemingly more skeptical than the supposed debtors. The downside of risk is the upside for a major gain. Contrarians can make money on gambles in the short run and the long term, if they keep all the variables in play. The value of vision is insight in an uncertain world, where overvalued gambles and bargains could pay off big. The gamble may not go your way every day, but with the economic beat plugged in for a pickup, the fund of information will continue to yield returns on investment.

It is amazing what you can accomplish if you do not care who gets the credit.

—Harry Truman

Chapter 4
Staying Legal

Integrity is not a 90 percent thing, not a 95 percent thing; either you have it or you don't.

—Peter Scotese

Rules and regulations can be our biggest obstacles as skip tracers. They sometimes pose a problem because we cannot do what we need to do in one maneuver. It is always important to stay within the law. No job or client is ever too big or too important to make you commit crimes. Many times you will be tempted to stray outside the law, but the end does not always justify the means.

Some time ago I had case for an attorney client representing a car dealership. John had a poor credit rating, and his brother Seymour agreed to cosign an installment agreement to buy a used car from his local car dealership. Seymour signed the contract on the line designated "Buyer" and John signed on the line designated "Co-Buyer." The contract went into default, and when my attorney client couldn't find the car or the skip for several months, they brought action for damages. Because they couldn't serve John, they proceeded against Seymour. But because Seymour was the guarantor in the contract, they would have to file suit against Seymour before they could proceed. The contract was plain and unambiguous, and there was no room for interpretation, even though it did not represent what the parties had intended it to mean. Seymour signed on the wrong line designated "Buyer," and therefore any reasonable person should have known that he was subjecting himself to primary liability for the purchase of the car. But because they had both signed the contract at the same time, they were both liable. When you apply common sense to a situation, you realize that even though you did not have the right to go after Seymour, in the end you did.

A planned-out strategy is the best method for reaching your goals; complying with the laws and regulations applicable to skipping is an absolute must and a first priority. For example, no pretext or deceptive practices can be used due to the GLB (Gramm–Leach–Bliley Act) and other federal privacy laws including the FCRA (Fair Credit Reporting Act), FDCPA (Fair Debt Collections Practices Act), and FACTA (Fair and Accurate Credit and Transaction Act of 2003), which are constantly being changed and/or amended. A partial text of the FDCPA and the GLB has been added in the bonus chapters at the end of the book for your reference.

Another general rule to keep in mind when tracking down deadbeats is that you must never identify the client or disclose the debt to a third party. This would be a breach of confidentiality. It could even lead to a conflict of interest, so choose your words wisely when communicating with third parties about the debtor. This is just one area you need to be aware of.

In Most Cases, the Regulations Governing Your Actions as a Skip Tracer Are Clearly Spelled Out

Let's take a look at some key terms and guidelines. We'll start with the issue of whether you need a license, and if so, what kind. Then we'll move on to staying in compliance with the Fair Debt Collections Practices Act, and we'll talk about issues of jurisdiction.

Licenses: Depending on which jurisdiction you are skip tracing in, a license may be needed. If you are doing surveillance or taking statements, as applied to contingent collections, licensing requirements will vary from state to state and county to county. Make sure to check with the local laws where you will be practicing.

Some states require a *private investigator license*, and others require a *collection agency license*, while others require both. Some states consider it a conflict of interest to have a private investigator involved in collections because generally collections are contingent, and private investigators are not supposed to work on a contingency basis, but rather on a retainer. It would also be difficult for a private investigator to be impartial if the outcome of the job depended on the results. Some states tax collections, and other states believe that collections have already been taxed. Private investigators in most states provide sales tax revenue at the state level. A private investigator is supposed to collect a retainer up front and charge sales tax, while a collector does not. *Champerty* is the practice of a third party participating in a lawsuit in order to share in the proceeds. Among laypersons, this is known as "buying into someone else's lawsuit."

It is important to know and understand which license you need. Private investigators investigate, while skip tracers research, but the two overlap. In fact, they are synonymous and share scope and responsibility. A private investigator can be construed as a researcher, but a researcher cannot be considered a private investigator because private investigators are licensed by the state and the researcher is not. A researcher can search all public record information. A private investigator is a detective and can perform many activities that researchers do not perform. For example, private investigators can serve process, they can take statements, they can do surveillance, they can perform background checks for any purpose, and in many states they are allowed to carry concealed weapons. The private investigator is a freelance detective who carries out covert investigations on behalf of private clients. Usually they are retired law enforcement personnel. They do not perform financial investigations.

Here are the definitions of *investigate* and *research as a compilation from the Internet*:

Investigate: To examine, study, or inquire into systematically; search or examine into the particulars of; examine in detail. To search out and examine the particulars of in an attempt to learn the facts about something hidden, unique, or complex, especially in an attempt to find a motive, cause, or culprit: The police are investigating the murder. To make inquiry, examination, or investigation. To follow up step by step, by patient inquiry or observation; to trace or track mentally; to search into; to inquire and examine into with care and accuracy; to find out by careful inquisition; as, to investigate the causes of natural phenomena. To make a detailed inquiry or systematic examination. To observe or inquire into in detail; examine systematically.

Research: Diligent and systematic inquiry or investigation into a subject in order to discover or revise facts, theories, applications, etc. A particular instance or piece of research. To make research; investigate carefully. To make an extensive investigation into: to research a matter thoroughly. Diligent inquiry or examination in seeking facts or principles; laborious or continued search after truth; as, researches of human wisdom. To search or examine with continued care; to seek diligently. Systematic investigation to establish facts. A search for knowledge. Scholarly or scientific investigation or inquiry. Close, careful study. The act of gathering information about a market or customer that will help progress or enable a sales approach.

It is a must to verify whether you are an investigator or a researcher. Once you determine which business type you are, contact your local licensing office and check to see if you need a license and, if so, which one you will need. Research is to see what everybody else has seen, and to think what nobody else has thought. It's a work in progress.

Always check with your local laws to make sure you are operating legally in your jurisdiction.

The Fair Debt Collections Practices Act is a very important regulation for skip tracers to understand In 1977, Congress enacted this in an attempt to curb what were perceived to be abuses by collection agencies. The act applies to specialized debt-collection agencies that, usually for a percentage of the amount owed, regularly attempt to collect debts on behalf of someone else. An example is debt buyers and collection agencies and collection attorneys, but not people collecting for themselves, such as a business collecting its own debts for itself. The FDCPA can be a bit of a stuffy subject, and in this ever-changing world, we need to understand how to comply. Let's start with the basics and then we'll go beyond.

If you are a new skip tracer, you need to understand the parameters that are allowed and the ones that are not allowed. Let's walk through a trace one step at a time. We have a phone number and an address for our debtor that we got from his original application from the transaction. When our debtor applied for something, like an apartment lease, a car loan, a credit card, or a mortgage, he filled out an application for credit. The first thing we want to do is verify if the information is still correct or if it is stale. There is a home number, a cell number, and a work number for him. The first thing we might want to do is call the phone numbers to see if they are still valid and if our debtor still lives there. But in order to comply with this law, we would not be able to call before 8:00 a.m. or after 9:00 p.m. We also might not be allowed to call the debtor at work if his employer does not allow it.

So before we go full blast and start dialing the phone numbers, we need to make sure that we are within the confines of the law. For each step we take, we will need to consider other variables to make sure we do it the right way and that we don't set ourselves up for any violations. One step cannot be determined before solving the prior step. So before we can call, we must first find out what time it is at that location and if the employer allows phone calls at work. Once we determine that, then we can take the next step, which is to call the number.

I have had many situations when I needed to verify employment, and when I called the employer, the person answering the phone said, "I am sorry. I cannot put you through to him because he is not allowed to get phone calls during work hours, but he gets his break at 3:30." That would probably be a violation, but sometimes we call the wrong office to verify, and human error is acceptable. Plus, I did not know he was not allowed to get calls during business hours.

As commercial dimensions and compliance codes change, good corporate citizens will need to innovate to stay current. In order to stay current, we need to understand the Fair Debt Collections Practices Act and how it applies to skip tracing. Enforcement of the act is primarily the responsibility of the Federal Trade Commission (FTC).

This federal legislation regulates the collection industry and its practices. The act allows debtors to recover civil damages, as well as attorneys' fees, in an action.

Creditors who attempt to collect a debt are not covered by the act unless, by misrepresenting themselves to the debtor, they cause the debtor to believe they are a collection agency. So if you collect for yourself, meaning if it is your own debt, the act does not apply to you.

The FDCPA applies only to the collection of debt incurred by a consumer for household or personal purposes primarily. One example of consumer debt is your personal telephone bill. If your telephone is a phone that is used exclusively for business, then it is a commercial debt, because your company would pay the bill for you. The act does not include commercial debt, unless the commercial debt has a personal guaranty. A personal guaranty is essentially what it sounds like, a guaranty from the person soliciting the loan/credit/contract on behalf of the entity.

Debt collections that are *not* covered by the FDCPA include the following:

- its own debts collected under its own name, or another institution's debts in isolated instances

- debts originated and then sold off, but that are still being serviced (like student loans and mortgages)

- debts that were not in default status when they were purchased

- debts that are factored (like accounts receivable financing)

- debts incurred as a result of a fiduciary responsibility or escrow arrangements

- debts for other institutions to which it is related by common ownership or corporate control

- debts that were obtained as security for commercial credit transactions

- debts collected by legal process servers

The act explicitly prohibits a collection agency from using any of the following tactics:

- contacting the debtor at the debtor's place of employment if the debtor's employer objects

- contacting the debtor during inconvenient or unusual times—before 8:00 a.m. or after 9:00 p.m. or at any time if the debtor is being represented by an attorney

- contacting third parties other than the debtor's parents, spouse, or financial advisor about payment of a debt unless a court authorizes such action

- communicating with the debtor at any time after receiving notice that the debtor is refusing to pay the debt, except to advise the debtor of further action to be taken by the collection agency and using harassment or intimidation such as abusive language or threatening violence or employing false or misleading information

- no impersonating a police officer or any government official or using any other unfair practice

The FDCPA requires validation of debt by providing the consumer, in writing:

- the amount of the debt

- the name of the creditor who is owed the debt

- notice that the consumer has thirty days to dispute the debt

- verification of the debt or a copy of the judgment; this is also known as validation of the debt

- if the original creditor is different from the creditor, notice that the consumer ma' the name and address of the origino

Contact with any third party in writing is allowed only if the envelope or content of the communication does not indicate the nature of the collector's business. No post cards are allowed because they disclose that it is related to a collection matter. Never disclose that the consumer owes any debt. The FDCPA preempts state law only to the extent the state law is inconsistent with the FDCPA.

These requirements are *not* too difficult to comply with. The regulations are a hassle to follow, but good corporate citizens will continue to abide by the laws and the rogue collectors will continue to abuse debtors. Everyone would like to be able to find and eliminate the sneaks who hide behind a legitimate business to break the law. But as we have seen before, a few rotten apples in a profession can ruin it for the whole industry. And the bullies will continue to bully the innocent unless we can trace them and weed them out.

With an increasing number of lawsuits filed in this year, we want to stay in compliance and stay away from unethical attorneys who "paper" collectors (file unnecessary paperwork) in order to create work for themselves to justify their existence. Should litigious debtors be "avoided" by collection firms? This would give litigants future benefits and is self-destructive because it creates a disservice to the client. Collectors should fund a protective legal defense against abusive FDCPA litigants to protect themselves from being abused, like a ush fund or a cleanup fund. These funds already exist. Seize every opportunity to protect yourself.

Every year, the number of FDCPA lawsuits that have been filed increases. Many thousands of businesses have been sued for violations over the past few years. There are about one thousand new lawsuits filed per month, based on the latest data, which makes the collection industry the largest growing industry for complaints (telemarketers are still in first place). Law firms that represent debtors are growing in numbers, and their case loads are increasing. Many law firms earn substantial fees suing or threatening collection agency companies for violations of the act. It has become more challenging than ever to comply, but there are always new approaches.

This is just a simple function of basic math—the worse the economy gets, the more files that are turned over for collection and the more lawsuits that are filed. So that if 100 files are turned over for collection, 17 suits would be filed, but if 1,000 cases are sent out for collection, then 170 law suits would be filed. Many debtors will just call the FTC and say that they got a collection call while they were playing a card game with friends and that makes it into the number of complaints. The FTC reports all calls that it receives, without verifying any information. They do not weed out the fake calls or duplicate calls. Each call is a statistic. Make a commitment to engage in constructive and respectful dialogue with consumers! My favorite approach is to gently advise them of the fact that they owe a debt, and we are here to help them through it.

FDCPA compliance is not a subject matter to take lightly. There are many attorneys who make a living by suing creditor rights attorneys, and the skip tracers who work for them who are also considered agents of the creditor. Whether they work directly or indirectly for the plaintiff, they must comply or face huge legal fees to defend these suits. At an average rate of $400 an hour for a lawyer to defend any action taken against the skip tracer or the creditor's attorney in a violation of the law, that adds up to big fees spent on defending yourself in the event of a complaint. Companies have set up shop just to teach collectors and skip tracers how to comply with the law. You can get educated further by taking classes and then get a certification that states that you and your skip tracers comply fully with this law. Insurance companies have set up policies to offer to collection agencies, attorneys, and skip tracers to be able to protect themselves in the event of an action taken against you or your agents or clients.

The successful skip tracer must know the ABCs of the FDCPA in order to stay in compliance with collection law. There are training videos, webinars, tutorials, books, software, and seminars on this topic for anyone who would like to dig deeper. We have seen critical issues and gained vital information to ensure compliance with the FDCPA. In today's skip tracer's world, researchers face battles that we have seen how to overcome.

When Tracing a Military Skip, It's Important to Comply with the Servicemembers Civil Relief Act

The Servicemember's Civil Relief Act provides a wide range of protections for individuals entering the military, called to active duty in the military, or deployed service members. The purpose is to delay or postpone certain civil obligations to enable service members to devote full attention to serving and reduce stress on the family members of those deployed service members. Some examples of these obligations they may be protected against are outstanding credit card debt, mortgage payments, pending trials, taxes, and terminations of lease.

The Servicemembers Civil Relief Act covers all active duty service members, reservists, and the members of the National Guard while on active duty. The protection begins on the date of entering active duty and generally terminates within thirty to ninety days after the date of discharge from active duty.

In addition, the new law expands the current law that protects service members and their families from eviction from housing while on active duty due to nonpayment of rents. It also provides a service member who receives permanent change of station orders or who is deployed to a new location for ninety days or more the right to terminate a housing lease. The new law also caps a 6 percent interest rate on existing debt while on active duty. This law only applies to debt incurred prior to military service.

Each branch of the military will do additional verification, so you will need to identify the branch as your first step, if you need additional information other than active or inactive duty status. Military personnel often function as communities within communities, by having their own military societies.

The general public may request records and information under the Freedom of Information Act, but not copies of entire records or personal information regarding former military service members. Information that is *not* available is personal recorded information about a member of the military, including:

- the individual's name, address, or telephone number

- the individual's race, national or ethnic origin, color, religion or political beliefs or associations

- the individual's age, sex, sexual orientation, marital status, or family status

- the individual's fingerprints, blood type, or inheritable characteristics

- information about the individual's health care status or history, including a physical or mental disability

- information about the individual's educational, financial, criminal, or employment status or history

- the opinions of a person about the individual

- the individual's personal views or opinions

For a military affidavit to be valid it must be current. The military search must be run within the last thirty days. We had an attorney who needed to serve a property execution by the time he made his motion in court and until the order was returned to him, so that he could proceed. Since forty-five days had passed, we had to do the military affidavit over again.

You will need to draw on extensive research to discover fascinating military insider details of the military players. Many of these master spies and spymasters are protecting our freedom and liberty, and that is why we need to protect those who protect us. Information may be accurate or misleading. If they can mislead the enemy in war, they are sophisticated enough to fool most skip tracers. If you go in knowing this in advance, it will make it easier for you to double check any missed security checks. Make the facts work for you so that you don't have to work so hard for the facts. Work smart not hard to maximize monetizing the information to work for you. Work less and live more.

Finally, reading between the lines is a must for every tracer. Every skip tracer must rely on his own powers of observation and be able to scan a vital document to pass it on to your checklist. With the technological advancements taking hold, methods and technology will expand as we evolve.

Jurisdiction Can Have a Profound Impact on the Success or Failure of a Skip Tracer's Efforts

A few weeks ago I had a client call and request an asset search. The client was a local business that had provided services to another business and had a personal guarantee from the debtor. He was not sure where the debtor was or even if they were still in the state. The client was not sure what to do, because if he could not find the debtors then he did not think he would be able to get his money. The client asked me to do a skip trace on the debtor but asked me what he should do once I found his debtor. I suggested that he go into court and get a judgment against them rather than assign it to a collection agency, because I thought they would be hard-core skips. The client asked me what good it would do him to get a judgment if the debtor was hard-core and probably wouldn't even show up in court, and then he wondered what on earth he would do with a default judgment.

I advised him that once he had that judgment, the picture changes and that court order would give him certain rights that he otherwise would not have. He was not sure that he understood, and I explained that once he got that judgment, that would give him recourse. He could take that judgment into wherever the debtor had his assets, and he could certify it and get his money through the court by using the legal process. This would also create a public record against the debtors and it would make it more difficult for them to cheat someone else later on.

Some laws are federal and some are local. It is when the two conflict with each other that the problems start. Judgments are public record, and those are governed by federal law. When you want to collect on the assets, you have to be careful to follow the local custom.

Jurisdictional challenges are most common when you get a judgment in one county or state and the debtor moves to another. But they can become very complicated when all sorts of variables are put into play.

Here are some examples of when jurisdictional issues become tricky and cross state lines:

- when a debtor works in one state but lives in another

- when a debtor lives and works in one state, but his employer is in a different state

- when a debtor lives in one state but has assets in another state

- when the debtor lives in one state, but he works in another state and his employer is in a third state and his assets are in a fourth state

As a general rule of thumb, you can certify your judgment in all the states where there are assets. This is whether you are an attorney or you are the judgment plaintiff. Otherwise, there are companies that provide these services for you. Skip tracers will sometimes do it on behalf of the client. This involves getting a certified copy of your judgment filed in the counties where there are assets. This process is referred to by some in the industry as *perfecting* your judgment. This procedure will allow you to execute against assets that are in those counties. This site is a great resource to search for every county nationwide and get map views from the National Association of Counties: http://www.naco. org/Template.cfm?Section=Find_a_County&Template=/ cffiles/counties/usamap.cfm.

Once you have determined where you need to serve papers, you can do that by visiting either one of these two websites that will guarantee superior serves:

http://www.napps.org/ This is the *National Association of Process Servers* and it an international network where licensed and bonded process servers are members. They are a worldwide organization of process servers that adhere to high ethical standards and are a collection of the most outstanding individuals in the profession.

www.serveamerica.com/ ServeAmerica is a source for locating process servers throughout America. Why outsource your nationwide process-serving needs? With ServeAmerica's process server directory, you can locate a local process server anywhere in the country. Legal professionals rely on the *Get a Quote* function and the exclusive ServeRATE process server rating system to ensure the highest quality service of process. A source provider to the information industry.

When Hiring a Process Server in Another State, Go with the Most Reputable One You Can Find to Avoid Ending Up in the Sewer Service Trap

Sewer service is term used for process servers who fail to properly serve lawsuit papers because of taking illegal shortcuts. One example of this is having one process server serve papers on someone in New York City and Buffalo at the same time, on the same date. The problem is that no one person can be at two places at the same time and have a notarized affidavit to prove it. The two cities are five hundred miles away. It is bad service.

This is a fraudulent business scheme in which companies allegedly fail to provide proper legal notification to thousands of people facing debt-related lawsuits, causing them to unknowingly default and have costly judgments entered against them without the chance to respond or defend themselves.

In the past, these process serving companies were hired by many high-volume debt collection law firms all over the country to serve collection lawsuit papers. This usually consisted of a summons and complaint which notifies consumers that they are being sued. Many companies often neglected to actually serve the papers as required by law, instead engaging in the highly illegal practice of *sewer service.*

As a result, many consumers were subsequently harmed when their bank accounts were restrained and their wages garnished. Many clients needed immediate bankruptcy protection because of this bad service. Since these consumers never knew they had been served, now a public record was created and default judgments had been entered against them without them knowing anything. They had never been given any notice. When they realized that they had become skips, they had to file for bankruptcy to get an automatic stay.

Sometimes due to bad service, a public record was created when there was no need for one. The consumer never got notice that he was served and the creditors made demands for payment so that the debtor had no choice but to file for bankruptcy protection to put a stay on calls from the lender.

The additional fraud that these companies committed was by covering up their illegal activity by falsifying documents and submitting them to courts across the states, swearing that proper legal notification had been duly served upon these individuals.

In addition, the process server's largest customers'—the high-volume debt collection firms—judgment papers became invalid for violations of states' consumer protection laws. According to the figures, some of these process servers served over twenty-eight thousand summons and complaints across the states, but failed to supervise the company and relied on legal papers from the process server that it knew or should have known were false. More than one hundred thousand records of affidavits of service were reviewed. Many of these debt collection firms that had all the judgments granted by these process server companies saw those judgments thrown out or vacated.

As a result of this, there has been a major shake-up in collections practices and the likelihood of numerous class-action suits. Process serving will never be the same. New regulations have just been set up where there were none before. It would be no surprise if some of the nation's largest collection law firms are driven out of business because of sewer service.

In the big scheme of things, regulations really do matter. Skip tracers need to be aware of the ones that play a role in the business, and it's important to keep up to date as regulations change. If you stay within the legal boundaries, you'll avoid costly lawsuits and hassles. It pays to know the score on the legal front.

In the middle of difficulty, lies opportunity.

—Albert Einstein

Chapter 5
Basic Intelligence Gathering

Skip tracing is all about putting information to work to accomplish the goal of finding the skip, even if he or she does not want to be found. To do an effective job means knowing how to gather data from a wide range of sources, assimilating that data, and drawing conclusions that lead to the skips and their hidden assets. Effective skip tracing also requires a systematic method when you go about collecting the data. It's helpful to have steps to follow, and I'll give you those steps in a little while. I've also included an excellent skip tracer's checklist for you to use, and in chapter 9 you'll find helpful links to my favorite databases (plus a whole lot more).

I can't emphasize enough that data is the fundamental building block of the skip tracer. It's the lifeblood of our business. Data is collected via sources, which can be classified into three broad groups—open source, closed source, and protected. Open-source information is public, and it's the easiest to get. Closed-source information is unprotected data that is not meant for public distribution, and it can be more difficult to get. Protected information is private, and it can be very difficult and sometimes illegal to get. Regardless of what sources you use, information gathering involves finding, selecting, and acquiring data and studying it to produce results. Skip tracing is a process created through mining, collecting, collating, and analyzing data for analysis as usable information to determine the whereabouts and location of your subject.

Using Open- and Closed-Source Data Is an Important Combination for Successful Skip Tracing

Open-source data: As noted, this is public information, or publically available information as opposed to covert or classified data. For example, anything in the public library, media, television, newspapers, blogs, social networking sites, and the Internet is open source intelligence. Government reports, official data such as budgets, demographics, hearings, legislative debates, press conferences, speeches, marine and aeronautical safety warnings, environmental impact statements, and contract awards are also open-source intelligence. Open-source intelligence in one term or another has been around for hundreds of years. A wide variety of vendors sell information products specifically within this category.

Closed-source data: As noted, this is nonprotected information. This is essentially "nonpublic" and includes information found in any government classification system that is not meant for general distribution. Closed sources are those not available to the public. People provide information based on their observations and conversations; an example of one could be a whistleblower. A professional tracer does not have to break any law or ask others to violate statues to be successful.

Protected data: Proprietary corporate information, an attorney's work product, or a person's medical records are all protected. Such information can be almost impossible to get legally.

Information is valuable, but not all data has the same value to us. If the information we gather does not apply to our goals, then it will be useless to us. What do we currently know? What don't we know? What do we need to know? What would we like to know?

Finding a Skip Requires Sticking to a Tried-and-True Method, Going Step by Step toward the Goal

Here's some things we should try to know about our subject. Check online directories and call the information operator at 411. If you have a telephone number for the skip, check the reverse telephone directories first and then call the number. Put the telephone number into at least three search engines. Make sure to put dashes between the numbers, use parentheses for the area code, and use periods. Repeat this process with all the variations in all three search engines. Format your search criteria like we described: (212) 555-5555 or 212-555-5555 or 212.555.5555 for best results.

If the last known address is an apartment building, check with the property management company to see if they have a forwarding address. Your subject may not have put in for a national change-of-address with the post office, but he did notify the property management company so that he would still get his monthly magazine subscriptions. Mail a letter to the last known address and view the information on the envelope after it is returned by the post office. Was the forwarding order expired? What does the information reveal? Check voter registration records. When was the last time that they voted? If the skip has school-aged children, check nearby schools. Check public schools, private schools, religious schools, parochial schools, independent schools, preschools, and nursery schools. Check with the power company. Inquire both by name and by last known address. Everyone needs electricity. Check with the water district. Inquire both by name and by last known address. We all need water and cannot live without it. Check with neighbors at the last known address. Check with family members.

If You Know the Skip's Profession, You May Be Able to Track Him or Her Down through a State License

Many professions require state licenses. Contact the appropriate licensing agency. Professions who are commonly licensed include:

- real estate agents

- real estate appraisers

- construction contractors

- insurance agents

- barbers and beauticians

- cosmetologists

- private investigators

- security guards

- doctors

- dentists

- accountants

- financial planners

- pharmacists

- nurses

- chiropractors

- engineers

- interior designers

These will vary from state to state, but most states have online access to this information. This is another great example of open-source data.

Many professions are unionized. Contact the appropriate labor union. Professions that are commonly union controlled include:

- government employees

- medical employees

- drivers

- air traffic controllers

- maritime jobs

- construction jobs

- auto workers

- mining workers

- electrical workers

- food workers

- hospitality

- most manufacturers

There are many more. Request the work history from the local union, for the current employment. This information is available through an information subpoena. The recipient must comply with the request. This is an example of closed-source data.

Real Estate and Motor Vehicle Information Often Provide Excellent Leads

Here are some more options to pursue. Real property is typically the most significant asset that an individual will ever own. Not only can you find the main residence an individual calls home, but you can also identify land adjoining their main residence, out-of-state vacation homes, and vacant land in the middle of nowhere. Motor vehicle registrations will not only reveal what car he is currently driving, but you may also even find a motorcycle. Watercraft registrations and vessels or boats are typically registered in a state; larger, more expensive boats must be registered with the US Coast Guard. Aircraft registrations could be checked, because all aircraft must be registered with the Federal Aviation Administration and can be registered by either individuals or companies. UCC filings are public information and are filed with the respective Secretary of State. UCC filings are typically backed by some sort of collateral. Civil litigation may identify a significant financial award, a settlement from an insurance company, or a former partner or a lawsuit that could disclose extensive stock holdings. Divorce proceedings are not public in every state divorce, but filings are available to the public in many states. Typically, divorce filings contain a net worth statement that includes details of bank account holdings, retirement funds, and other assets.

Probate filings should be checked to see if an inheritance from a relative or a grandparent can be identified. Identifying key family members and distant relatives who recently passed away can lead to an inheritance. Corporate filings and ownership in a corporation, a limited liability company, or a limited partnership may be the key to identifying assets not held directly in the party's name. With private companies, it may be difficult to fully understand the value of the business because detailed information is not typically available on closed companies. The business may have real property, vehicles, equipment, or patents registered in the individual's name.

SEC filings are required for publicly traded companies, which are required to make certain disclosures that private companies are not. These disclosures may include stock options to executives, significant stock holdings, compensation, or even independent contractor agreements with related parties. Patents and trademarks and intellectual property rights should be checked for real assets that could potentially be worth millions. Nonprofit entities and charitable entities need to be traced when you are thinking about assets. Assets may have been diverted to a nonprofit that is funneling money back to the target individual through expense payments or salary payments and other awards. Small business retirement accounts are assets that must be checked. If the party you are looking into owns a business, he may have put a large portion of its earnings into the company's retirement plan. Small businesses are required to file an annual Form 5500 with the IRS that provides information about the funds. Business affiliations should be examined. Your debtor may not have any assets held directly in his or her name, but he may be holding assets under a business trust to insulate himself from prying eyes.

A Skip's Assets Can Be Hidden in Trusts, Business Retirement Funds, or Offshore

In addition to searching for corporate affiliations for your subject, corporations can be set up in trusts, or with family members or close business associates. These are also called trusted associates. States like as Delaware give special tax treatment and priority and favorable treatment to corporations and maintain anonymity.

Overseas assets should not be overlooked, because stashing assets abroad is a common way to hide assets. While international banking regulations may prohibit you from obtaining bank records, items such as real property, boats, corporations, or, in some cases, income tax records may be publicly accessible. There is no comprehensive way to search for assets internationally unless you know where to look and what countries your subject may have traveled to.

Follow These Steps When Gathering Open- and Closed-Source Intelligence:

1. Run the Social Security number through all your databases and analyze the results.

2. Do a reverse address; look up to see who else is living with your subject.

3. Run the people that live at the address. Skips move back with family, and kids go home to their parents.

4. When you find a phone number for the skip, call the number. If the debtor picks up, say "I am sorry. I dialed the wrong number. Sorry to trouble you."

5. Check voter registration records. I have almost never seen a voter registration address listed as a post office box. It will also tell you the last time your skip voted.

6. Pull a Department of Motor Vehicle (DMV) report to see if your skip bought a new vehicle or to see if his license is suspended. Check for new registration. Look for when the registration expires. The site www.Carfax.com has the last date that the car had a state inspection. You can find the location of the inspection station, and call the station and request any information on file.

7. Check marriages and divorces. When a skip totally disappears and has no inquiries on his credit reports, I think he is incognito. But sometimes they just got married. Your skip may have also dropped the maiden name. The same change of name happens in divorce situations.

8. Look for pending litigation and lawsuits. People who have sued your skip, have information. They need information on your skip because they want to get paid. Creditors stick together.

9. Search your local, state, and county government. Con artists usually have several "doing business as" (DBA) entries registered in their name. Check the Secretary of State. Is your skip self-employed? Look for information on the Better Business Bureau (BBB) website www.bbb.org. A complaint could get you a new lead. I have found bank accounts through them.

10. Call the last property management office for the address where the refund of deposit was sent to. If they skipped out, you may be able to get the "in case of emergency" number and see who they lived with. Try searching for the associate. Many times when I can't find my skip, I look for the spouse or family member instead.

11. Check for a change of address by sending mail. "ADDRESS SERVICE REQUESTED" should be

printed in bold caps under your return address. If a forwarding order has been submitted by your debtor, you will get that forwarding order back in the mail in about three weeks.

12. Look at the address on the driver's license. Search for your skip by name and date of birth to make sure you have covered that avenue. I have been able to validate my skip from the date of birth and name, *not* address.

13. Run property records to help you locate family members who own their home. The family always knows how to reach them. My father always knows how to get me on the phone. Don't your parents know how to get a hold of you?

14. Run a professional license check. Every state has different laws for regulating state licenses. If your skip has worked in a profession, check to see if there is a license for that; you might get a new address and a job.

15. Your social media search should scrub the Internet for your skip. It should give you every possible link to your skip. Snoop doggin' all the way through in all the social media spaces or you can always use one of the programs like www.hootsuite.com for that.

16. Check parking tickets. Unpaid tickets are converted into state, city, and county warrants. Those are loaded with information. In most cities' online site, anyone can log on with their driver's license number and pay their tickets. A new address and phone number could be found.

17. Run a criminal search to see if your skip is in jail or on parole.

18. Run a military search to see if your skip is deployed. That will give you a date range and let you plan your next step.

A checklist helps busy tracers stay on course. It organizes debtor files and improves case reviews. I've included below a step-by-step checklist you can use when gathering intelligence on skips. The list will never be complete because everything echoes endlessly on. Not all of these will apply to your needs every time, but maybe it will give you some ideas and you can add them to the list. Make sure that every stone has been turned and every crack has been checked for information to help locate your debtor. Skip tracing is a game of hide-and-seek, in a sense. The debtor is hiding, you are seeking—it's that simple! If he is hiding from you, then he is probably hiding from someone else. Analyze your information effectively to plan your strategy wisely.

Skip Tracer's Checklist

Note: The checklist below is featured in our webinar and can be downloaded at the following link: http://www.searchnetmgt.com/downloads/SearchNet-SkipTracersChecklist.doc

SKIP TRACER'S CHECKLIST

Preinvestigative Checks

- City Directory

- Directory Assistance

- Postal Forwarding Address Check

- Multiples

- Date of Birth

Public Record or Courthouse Records Check

- Traffic Records

- Circuit Civil Records

- County Civil Records

- Circuit Criminal Records

- County Criminal Records

- Voter Registration

- Marriage Records

- Occupational License

- Property Tax Rolls

- Hunting and Fishing Licenses

- Real Property Records

- Auto Tag Registration

- General Indexing

<u>Last Known Address</u>

- Neighbors Interviewed

- Local Area Merchants Contacted

- Landlord [ ] yes [ ] no

- Real Estate Agent [ ] yes [ ] no

- Names of Other Members of the Household

- Moving Company [ ] yes [ ] no

Deposits

- Landlord

- Gas Company

- Cable Company

- Electric Company

- Telephone Company

- Garbage Pick-up Service

State Records

- Auto Tag

- Driver License

- Vehicle Title

- Corporate Names

- State Occupational License

- State Highway Patrol

- State Disciplinary Actions

Other Assorted Checks

- Interviews with Relatives [ ] mother [ ] father [ ] sisters [ ] brothers [ ] grandparents [ ]aunts and uncles [ ] cousins [ ] stepfamilies

- Employer

- Former Employers

- Labor Unions

- Schools

- Magazine Subscriptions

- Organizations

- Church or Temple

- Door-to-Door Salesman from Last Known Address

- Former Spouse

- Children

- Out-of-Town Friends

<u>Other Leads and Notes</u>

Databases Play a Crucial Role in Intelligence Gathering

There are free databases and there are subscription databases. Some are good and some are great. All are necessary, and without them, we would be in the days of the dinosaurs. Databases have taken a job that was once extremely difficult, time-consuming, and costly into something that is a breeze. Databases are all different and many times report conflicting information. The most important step that the skip tracer can take is to verify the information on the database. Once you have called and verified that the information is correct, only then can you go to the next step.

Databases, like libraries, have different information filed in different locations for ease of use. For example, libraries will have all of the history books in one section and the cooking books in another. If we want birth and death records, we will go into one section, but if we want historical ownership of properties, we will go into another part of the library or database. Just like in our own computers, we keep similar things together. For example, our e-mail is in one program, but our pictures are in another place. When we need to search for something, we look where it belongs. The "find" feature will not look through every single item on your computer. It would be too much to plow through.

This is one of my favorite topics because databases are a great place to start, but they are not an end-all. Think about the source of the information which is public records. The researchers go into the courthouses and government sources and pick up the info, then they reformat and repackage it for resale. Or in many cases, it is done electronically through a digital transfer. So the most import task is to be able to verify it and make sure it is correct and accurate. Otherwise it is worthless and useless information.

The Major Credit Reporting Agencies Are Great Sources on Businesses That Receive Ratings

Our skip-trace tools used on a daily basis include the three major credit bureaus. When trying to locate people, the credit bureaus often have the most up-to-date address, phone, and employment information.

Even though the information is similar, different databases have different results because there are different ways of viewing things. There's the perspective thing again.

Think about the term *draining customer*. Does that mean you are the drain or you are being drained? It's the perspective. There are at least two ways to see it and many more than that. This is also known as managing perception or perception management. Advanced skip tracing means going beyond the databases and seeing the bigger picture—being able to see the whole forest without getting caught up in the trees.

You can use Dun & Bradstreet or Hoovers to see if a person owns a business or where they work. D&B is a subscription database. You must sign up and get a contract with them directly, or you can access the information through an information provider. If you do open an account, it is costly, but worth every penny. They have an "Executive Search" by state. Enter the first name and last name and pick your state, then check for all types of businesses. The results will show you all the businesses that your subject is affiliated with. Check each company report for additional information like public records, UCC filings, intercompany transactions, property, and much more. Hoovers is now owned by D&B and they feed off similar information. I have seen information on Hoovers that was not in D&B and the other way around, but I always think of them as the skip tracer's best friend. I do not believe they are available to the general public other than a name search, so they will let you know if they have the information for your skip and then you can order it through your information broker. Do not confuse this search with a credit bureau search for a consumer. These are credit reports for businesses only. They do not rate individuals.

Individual Credit Reports Are Protected Data and Require Special Circumstances to Gain Access, such as When a Collection Agency Seeks the Information on a Deadbeat Account

Credit bureau reports for consumers can only be pulled for permissible purpose. For instance, if a collection agency was looking to collect on a judgment or a delinquent account, this would give them permissible purpose to run a credit report. They also report delinquent accounts to the credit bureaus. In a case where you are applying for a job, you will need to sign a written release for them to be able to pull a credit report on you. In a landlord/tenant case where you are applying to rent an apartment, the management company would need your signature in order to run a credit report on you. There are different types of credit reports for different purposes, and even though the information is the same, it is presented differently. For example, if you were applying for a job or your employer was running a background check on you, your account numbers would not be shown. But if you were a collection agency, they will give you more information and a partial account number. The credit report for employment purposes would show that you are paying "as agreed," but the collection report would say thirty, sixty, or ninety days so that you could figure out how fast or slow they are paying. You are entitled to a free credit report every year. You can get your free credit report at www.annualcreditreport.com. They will not give you your FICO score, and if you need that to determine if you are eligible for low rates, you can get that at www. freecreditreport.com.

Websites like Amazon.com Can Yield Intriguing Results

Don't forget to check out the invisible web with sites like www.Amazon.com because you can bank on it. At my last seminar, one of my students asked how we searched for assets in Amazon.com. To site one example, if you know the person is an author, then you would search for the books on the website. Once you find the book, then you could search for a royalty account, because you know that authors get paid for their work in the form of royalties. Once you know that funds are going into some kind of account, it is your job as a skip tracer to find where that account is. If you did not know that they had something for sale on the site, then you would miss the asset. Not too long ago I had a case where an author had passed on, and he had several psychology and self-help books available for sale at the time of his passing. His latest book was coauthored with his wife, and she knew where that royalty account was. It was my job to figure out what other accounts he had at the time of death, because those royalty payments were going into another account. I could have gone the long route and gotten the information with an information subpoena, but it was faster to check with the existing bank first, and that was exactly where the other accounts were. That was a hidden asset because it was an online account with an electronic direct deposit.

Before we get into some of the most basic intelligence gathering resources, I need to point out that there are two different types of databases—columnar and decision support.

Columnar databases: This management system stores data in columns instead of rows. It is also a tabular format.

Decision support databases: This is a database from which data is extracted and analyzed statistically in order to inform us. There is also *cloud computing* which is when a database is accessible to clients from the cloud (where information is stored) and delivered to users on demand via the Internet from a cloud database provider's servers. With so many different flavors it becomes hard to choose.

When Searching a Database, Make Sure What You Type In Is Accurate or You'll Lose a Lot of Time

Make sure to double check when inputting data, because small mistakes can cost big bucks. Also double check the information provided by the client. For example: Michelle Daniel versus Daniel Michelle. Just by transposing those two names, we have created entirely different people. Now let's put another variable into play: the person uses Dan, Danny, Danille, Dannie, Danney for a nickname, but the real name is Daniel. You will have a harder time verifying the information. When you enter the data, if all the variables don't match, many times certain databases get confused and you get a "No Record Found." This happens often if you put in the city and state and enter the wrong zip code for the state; the algorithm can't find it and your results yield no fruit. While computers are machines that are programmed or trained to think like humans, they get disoriented just like we do. Try not to confuse them!

Below are some basic resources every skip tracer will use to gather intelligence on a skip.

Credit bureau reports: The preferred resource of the skip tracer is the credit report. Because the consumer profile is created for measuring creditworthiness, it provides the most accurate information for skips. They were created by the creditors to measure the amount of risk the lender should take with the consumer, based on past performance or history that is rated with a risk score and other credit risk models. Skip tracers prefer the Hawk

Alerts, change-of-address dates, alerts, monitoi
notification service, line-of-credit accounts, "in fil
additional names and Social Security numbers, (
inquiries, types of inquiries, and consumer state   _.. .u.
These are public record. While all three bureaus have
almost the same information, most skip tracers have their
personal preference. You'll have to decide which one
you like best.

Secretary of State: This instrument allows us to search
for businesses, employers, and in many states also by the
agent or principal. Each state has different guidelines and
models. All slates offer customer service by telephone
during business hours.

County clerk's office: This function is best used
for verifying a business license. Many counties are
not searchable online, and a manual search by an
experienced court researcher is advised because some
books contain manual entries that must be deciphered,
and a knowledge of the local courthouse custom is a
definite advantage. The costs for these depend on the
county. They vary and the least expensive way is to use a
service that specializes in this because they have expert
court researchers available nationwide.

Tax assessor's office: This technique is used to find
out the last time taxes were paid on the property and
who paid them. Sometimes properties are put into family
trusts and a trust identification number is needed. This is
one source for that information. The results of this search
can yield hidden assets.

City clerk's office: The system dictates that this office issues all vendor and peddler licenses. These instruments contain a wealth of personal information and can be subpoenaed. Most cities are available online.

Driver's license records: These tools can be ordered through your online vendor. Key information that tracers look for is whether the license is expired or active and what type of license is it. The type of license will get you whether he is a driver or an operator. If he is an operator, then that means you've probably got an asset. If the license is expired or suspended, was it for nonpayment? That can also get you another asset with a subpoena. These records are not open to the public and in some states like Georgia they are only open to law enforcement. Most information providers sell this information. In order to open an account, you will need to have a site inspection to verify you are a real business and comply with all the rules and regulations.

Motor vehicle registration records: This method gets you information about whether the vehicles are insured and if there are any lien holders on the vehicles. There is a wealth of information that can be obtained from the Department of Motor Vehicles.

Telephone books: While currently out of favor in the current cyberspace climate, *keep all old telephone books*. When data is lost or compromised, the hard data is as valuable as the hard assets. They are a treasure in themselves.

Directory assistance: This program is worth the fee. Because websites and directories are updated bimonthly, the most up-to-date information will, as we learned in previous chapters, be available from the source. In this case, the source is the telephone company, which is the custodian of records.

City directories: This resource is one of the best tools available, and it would be great if all cities had them. The directories contain residents, occupations, and businesses in town, head of households, and much more, depending on the city. Some cities don't have them.

US Post Office: This federal agency will allow you to request a forwarding address. They have the form on file at your local branch, and the response time is up to two weeks. If they have it, you can get it.

Cross reference directories: For well over a century, Polk directories have made finding information easier and more efficient. And now, their nationwide city directory is a service of infoUSA, a trusted and loved source provider to the information industry. Print versions are no longer cost efficient, but their DVDs and CDs are primo—costly but worth the bucks for the connoisseurs.

Military directories: Because lawyers are required to comply with the Soldiers and Sailors Act during times of war, we need to verify if the subject is on active duty. There is no one repository of information for all the branches of the military, so you will need to check each branch separately to find out what the correct procedure will be to get the information you need.

Internet: The front-runner by popularity and the number-one source of information is the World Wide Web. It is important to know and understand how the net works in order to maximize its utility. This is a fluid medium, and it is forever changing. From one second to the next, headlines and stories change. With the blogs and social sites online, the resources are unlimited, literally. If you understand the concept of infinity, you know that it just goes on and on. The way the web works is by cataloging information that the web bots or web crawlers ferret out. These spiders go out to pick up the mood of the web, then catalog all the words in an indexed table, and then log the websites that those words appear on. To imagine a broader image would be a simple table with other added variables and cumulative probabilities that include timing since the web is constantly changing. When we Google a term, that search engine sends out an algorithm looking for that term on websites.

Cartography: This incredibly rich information is based on movements and behaviors of cell phones and mobile devices. These are powered by a bunch of algorithms that turn mountains of data into intelligence. With a geo-tracking feature, they can share location data with friends and family if you are stuck in traffic. Cloaking is available. This means that if you want, you can turn off the feature and you will be shielded from anyone knowing your location. As landlines become obsolete, people move to innovative cost-saving techniques. It is equal to the change when people went from adding machines to calculators or from tellers to ATMs. It was a big improvement in quality of life. These applications are already available on the new Google phones, IT phones, and most other telecom providers. Four Square is the market leader for these geo-tracking features. This is a great feature for anyone who loses their phone, because you will now be able to recover it. All things are possible to the person who believes they are possible.

Cyber tracking: *Cyber* is from the Greek word for navigator. Cyber tracking is the real-time tracking of all activity on the Internet or in cyberspace, the electronic medium in which online communication takes place. It means tracking someone on the Internet. It also applies to tracking vehicles, trailers, motorbikes, boats, caravans, motor homes, and personnel. The Internet allows cyber stalkers to follow and harass victims anonymously from anywhere. This is your secret weapon for skip tracing. Cyber stalkers can be like cyber attacks.

Basic intelligence gathering is all about using every resource you have available to track down the subject of your investigation and to find those hidden assets. As you can see, you've got plenty to work with, so no matter how clever the skip is, you should be able to outsmart the fox!

Nurture your mind with great thoughts, for you will never go any higher than you think.

—Benjamin Disraeli

Chapter 6
Gems in the Dumpster

Too many people miss the silver lining because they're expecting the gold.

—Maurice Setter

We've all heard about Dumpster diving. Typically, it involves a homeless person climbing into a Dumpster to hunt for food, or a criminal poking around to see if you were dumb enough to throw out bank statements and other private information that could be used for identity theft. The skip tracer uses Dumpster diving too, and there are definitely legal and ethical issues involved that we need to explore. Likewise, we sometimes use clever ways to gather intelligence, and some of them fall into gray areas of the law. Other practices that can be used for intelligence gathering are absolutely, positively illegal. You need to know what they are so you stay on the right side of the law.

We'll discuss the key areas of more advanced intelligence gathering in this chapter. With these techniques, you're dancing close to the realm of the traditional private investigator and away from the more typical research functions that make up much of a skip tracer's day.

Garbage Tells Skip Tracers Plenty, and It's Often Easily Accessible and Legal to Search

As I've said, one source of information for both the criminal and the skip tracer is the garbage. The criminal looks for personal information such as Social Security numbers, account numbers, and other things we'll look at shortly, and the skip tracer looks for gold nuggets. In most states, when garbage is put out on the street, the person who threw it out has no expectation of privacy to it. That means free pickin's for anyone willing to put on rubber gloves and a mask. Recently, more companies have set up shop to practice "garbology," which is a study by analyzing garbage.

Unless the garbage was disposed of in a Dumpster in a gated community, it becomes public domain in most communities nationwide. If it is physically located inside of someone's property, you could be trespassing. But if it is out on the street for pickup, it has no expectation of being private property. In a recent decision, the US Supreme Court held that there is no common law expectation of privacy for discarded materials.

Dumpster diving is the practice of sifting through commercial or residential trash that has been discarded by their owners to find things that may be useful to the Dumpster diver. The practice of Dumpster diving is also known variously as urban foraging, binning, alley surfing, curbing, D-mart, Dumpstering, garbaging, freeganism, garbage picking, garbage gleaning, skip-raiding, skip diving, skipping, skip-weaseling, tatting, skally-wagging, or trashing. The term *Dumpster diving* originates from the best-known manufacturer of commercial trash bins—Dumpster—and the fanciful image of someone leaping headfirst into a Dumpster as if he or she was diving into a swimming pool. In practice, the size and design of most Dumpsters makes it possible to retrieve many items from the outside of Dumpsters without having to "dive" inside.

All too often, Dumpsters can be an inadvertent (for the owner) source of information. Unwanted files, letters, memos, photographs, IDs, and other paperwork have been found in Dumpsters. This oversight is a result of many people not realizing that sensitive items like passwords, credit card numbers, and personal information they throw into the trash could be recovered anywhere from the Dumpster to the landfill. This recovered information is sometimes used by criminals for fraudulent purposes, such as identity theft and the breaking of physical information security. Information to most Dumpster divers is unusable, and if the items found are unusual such as stolen wallets, purses, or Oscars, sometimes these items are turned over to the police or their owners if it has no byproduct usability.

Targeted information diving was more common in the 1980s due to poor security. When businesses became aware of the need for increased security in the early

1990s, it became routine for sensitive documents to be shredded before being placed in Dumpsters. Security mythology still portrays the stereotypical lone hackers or malicious crackers commonly searching through office waste, but this may be more of an urban legend because social engineering is often easier, more productive, and is a more predictable source than Dumpsters. But criminals' methodology overlaps or conflicts with security mythology. Every skip tracer must rely on his or her powers of observation and recall, because as technology advances, so do methods and equipment for more effective surveillance.

Information diving is a legal source for obtaining financial information, including account numbers. Shame on you if you threw it out in the garbage. That is what shredders are for. If you threw it away without shredding, you are inviting trouble. You almost deserve to get your identity stolen or your banking information compromised.

If You've Tracked Down a Debtor's Address, a Dive into the Dumpster Might Turn Up Evidence of Hidden Assets

If you're going through someone's trash, you know who and where they are. The trash could be a great place for the skip tracer to find evidence of a hidden asset on the one who threw out the garbage. I have actually gone Dumpster diving on one case. I did find the bank statements that I needed in the garbage. It was dangerous because it was late at night in a bad neighborhood, but I was lucky I did not have to wait all night till the garbage was put out in the morning. It was a dirty and smelly job—the garbage was coated with coffee grounds, but I got the information I needed. I have also used companies that have people who specialize in doing this. I have almost never been disappointed with the results. I think this is the one step that you will need to experience yourself at some point in your skip tracing career.

Trash dips, trash audits, and *garbology* are other terms used for this popular tool that the skip tracer may need to resort to. When on the slippery slope of self-doubt, this method will usually exceed your expectations and deliver riches.

Advanced Intelligence Gathering Often Requires Working in Gray Areas of the Law

Gray areas are undefined situations, subjects, or fields not readily conforming to a category or existing set of rules. It is an indeterminate territory, undefined position, neither here nor there. There's a large gray area between what is legal and what is not. This term uses *gray* in the sense of neither black nor white, or right or wrong. *Gray area* also refers to the hidden and mysterious or obscure. This space is sometimes dark and questionable but always a step the skip tracer must calculate to prepare for the obstacles up ahead. Gray area does not necessarily mean anything is against any law. What is hidden or gray is legal, but we don't need to show it openly.

For example, a sting is usually reserved for difficult locates. Many members of the National Association of

Process Servers, or NAPPS, have to set up subjects to get them served every day. When the subject avoids service, you'll need to play by their rules. Since they don't want to make themselves available, if they have a business or are in a position of service, call them and offer to buy something from them. Set up an appointment for a sales meeting; then when they come or when you go—bingo, you got them.

That said, I would be remiss in my duty if I did not warn you that undercover work can be dangerous. As soon as you leave the office and head out into the field, you put yourself at risk. There are some really crazy people out there, and if you are a skip tracer you will run up against some of them. Let me share a short and sad story about a case I was on years ago that demonstrates just what can happen during the course of what should have been a routine day.

The case involved a landlord in Brooklyn. The landlord owned several small buildings in the Bedford Stuyvesant section. She had problems collecting rent and evicting the tenants for nonpayment of rent. Sometimes the landlord and others like her were tied up in court proceedings, trying to get the rent that was owed to them. This was a very costly and time-consuming process that drained the landlord of all her working capital and eventually hurt her because she did not have the liquidity to pay her taxes and bills. A city marshal was trying to serve papers and an eviction notice to the tenant living on the second floor of this three-story brownstone. When the marshal got to the door to serve the tenant, he was killed when an argument escalated into a vicious fight outside the apartment.

Apparently, the tenant sprayed the marshal with some kind of aerosol spray and then shot him to death before lighting him on fire. The marshal's .38-caliber Glock semiautomatic was found on the stairwell near his body. He never even had the chance to fire it and protect himself. Someone in the building called the police, and they came immediately. The police searched the neighborhood with dogs and detectives with no luck, until the tenant walked calmly up to the officers who were stationed at the crime scene and turned himself in. The marshal was just to deliver court papers and padlock an apartment door, and he lost his life. It was this deadly and tragic day that made me realize just how dangerous the marshal's job really is. And how dangerous mine is when I go into the field to do more advanced intelligence gathering. Always be careful. Never put yourself at risk if you don't have to. Losing your life over a skip is just not worth it.

When in Doubt, Staying on the Ethical Side of a Skip Trace Is the Only Way to Go

There is a difference between unethical and ambiguous. What is clear is that there is a right way and a wrong way to do things. That will apply to both life and skip-tracing tasks. For our purposes, ethical will equate with legal. We can all be assured that the skip will be hunted down with ethical methods. It might cost more now that we need to take several steps in order to accomplish our hunt, but the hunt will go on, and the prey will be had for best pickings. One of skip tracing's finer points is to know that you should not react before you've had a chance to think. Be prepared, and go in with all the facts at your fingertips so that you are ready for anything. Don't confuse illusion with delusion.

Tracking down vital information to report back to the client is like using intelligence to stay ahead of the skip. In reality it is like a skip tracer becoming an expert on tactics and execution. Skip tracers are fascinating and their work fuels a million fantasies, including taking on a false identity and working undercover in great danger to assure victory. In the skip tracer's world, courage, determination, and the ability to think quickly on your feet are basic ingredients. One formula for success includes being adept at getting a person to disclose information without realizing that they are being questioned, while keeping in the back of your mind that they might be trying to intentionally give you misleading information. Many times when people divorce and custody battles run rampant, a jealous spouse might ask the children, "What did you do this weekend?" The children tell them everything they did all weekend and with whom and how much they spent and if they used a debit card or paid for everything in cash. I see this in my work on a regular basis, when the parent says they had a visitation with the spouse last weekend, and the children told them they had to stop at a new bank to pick up cash. As a skip tracer, you will be able to see things that you never thought of before, because in this discipline you must learn to see things from different sides. It is almost like magic.

Assessing the information must be accurate and timely. Always try to take a step back from your personal perspective and see the bigger picture. Subjectivity is acceptable and encouraged when choosing between a cheesecake and a chocolate cake; the recipes for each will be as different as night and day, and the procedures for making each are also uncorrelated. So keep these thoughts in the back of your mind when doing a final assessment.

Don't Misrepresent Who You Are, but Do Use the Subtleties of Mood, Language, and Setting to Prime a Subject to Give You the Information You Need for Your Client

Whenever possible, use the "mood" to get what you want. This is one of those hidden secrets that people are afraid to talk about, but suggestion works well when you can set up this scenario. When you place a call and a child answers the phone, they usually are unsuspecting and don't ask who it is. You can ask, "What time will Mom be home?" or, "Is Mom still at work?" The answer should open all sorts of doors and yield all kinds of hidden assets.

According to business.com, it is a fact that over 30 percent of US households have abandoned landline phones. Almost everyone has a cell phone. Almost every cell phone can receive text messages. At least 96 percent of text messages are read. Almost all of the responses are within thirty minutes. As a skip tracer, you simply send a text to that number. Then just wait and see what happens. Did you get a response? Was the text ignored? Did the text bounce? This step in itself will yield plenty of gems. Make sure to leave no gem unturned. I get wrong numbers and wrong texts all the time, and I am not hiding out from anyone. These text messages are FDCPA and *Telephone Consumer Protection Act* (TCPA) compliant and can be autodialed and free to the end user. The future of successful collections and skip tracers belongs to the most innovative.

You don't have to peek in someone's medicine cabinet to know something about them anymore. Instead, you can look on their medical chart. While a medical record is protected information, sometimes under the doctor/patient privileged communications, information must be reported to the authorities. One example of this is the recent case where a mentally ill twenty-four-year-old man opened fire in a movie theater in Aurora, Colorado, killing or wounding almost seventy people. At this point, his medical history is the subject of state investigators and skip tracers conducting the investigation on behalf of the state.

But the hospitals have it even easier. In the past, hospitals weren't allowed to run credit reports. Nowadays, if you don't have health insurance, hospitals are allowed to run a check to see if you are a good credit risk. If your credit is poor, the hospital may not tend to you right away or even at all because they may not get paid for their services. Under the doctrine of unjust enrichment, they are not required to provide service to you, other than to their oath to the medical profession. This has resulted in lowering bad-debt expenses for the hospitals at the expense of the American patient.

While It Might Be Tempting to Step over the Legal Line, the Consequences Don't Merit the Potential Gains

After you've gone Dumpster diving, set up a sting or two, and lulled an unsuspecting person into innocently divulging information about a skip, you'll have begun your transformation from a beginner to an advanced skip tracer. Our business is focused mostly on research, but we do get out of the office to hunt in the field. That's one of the more exciting parts of our work. Rest assured that there will come a time when you feel you're inches from getting the information you need to locate a treasure trove of hidden assets, but you can't figure out how to close the deal within the confines of the law. When that happens, and it will, take a few steps back and consider what you're doing. As I've said, you need to stay on the right side of the law. If you don't, you get down in the mud with your skip, and that's a bad thing.

In order for you to see what I'm talking about in more depth, I'm going to explore some intelligence-gathering methods and techniques that are in violation of certain state and federal laws. It is not my intention to promote or encourage anyone to break the law, but rather, to instruct and illustrate techniques which were once used before they became illegal due to privacy laws.

Pretexting: This is the art of obtaining information from either the subject or a third party without letting them know that you are gathering information. There are two basic types of pretexts: positive and negative. A positive pretext is one in which the target is given a positive reason to talk to you—a reward. The negative pretext is one in which the target is given a negative reason to talk to you—fear or panic. The type and style or shape and size of the ruse you use is up to you. You are only limited by your acting ability and your imagination. Some say that a good skip tracer is like an actor whose script is a pretext. You can use anything in your arsenal of acting skills to help make your pretext real—use accents, backgrounds, or whatever is appropriate to the stage. The more real the subject believes this pretext is, the more information you will obtain. You must become a good actor and believe in your ability. This is a very powerful tool to act out a piece of artwork. Telemarketers are a perfect example of pretexters. They call us to try to sell us something under the pretext that they have the best offer in the world for us if we switch and use them.

The Federal Trade Commission reported in that several private investigators who were involved in a boardroom spying case at Hewlett-Packard Co. will pay $600,000 in settlements and judgments to settle the case. A complaint was filed last year by the FTC because the investigators allegedly illegally obtained private phone records (also called "pretexting"), using methods like the ones we just described. The investigators were hired by Palo Alto–based Hewlett-Packard in 2005 to examine private telephone logs of journalists, board members, and company employees in order to find the source of leaks to the media.

On the other hand, you've got to make a choice as a skip tracer. What might strike some as a pretext won't strike others the same way. For example, is there anything wrong with calling someone and asking them, "What is your favorite newspaper?" and as a byproduct get their address? Has someone lied? I do not think there is anything wrong with trying to authenticate someone or something by asking a simple question that has nothing to do with privacy or personal information. Is it a pretext to go into someone's business and purchase something with a check, and as a byproduct get the bank account information, including account number? It is 100 percent legal.

Roping: This is the investigative term for a method where you *induce* a person or persons to reveal the desired information without them realizing that any information has been revealed. Elements of roping intermingle with elements of the pretext, so much so that often it is difficult to distinguish between the two. Roping is an expression that means to draw out from an individual the information, as if with a rope. Usually a roping operation will be of longer duration than a pretext. Unlike a pretext, though, a rope must be planned out with defined guidelines, or it will not work. Do not confuse this with a setup or sting. Roping is a little bit like enticement. Think about an alcoholic, if you put a drink out in front of them they may not be able to resist the temptation. They may fall victim to temptation. The same holds true for someone on a diet; if you put food out on the table, they may get roped into eating it. You can also think of roping figuratively like when you sling a rope around a horse to bring him in or catch him.

This method will need persistence, and there is no substitute for persistence. Concentrate your thoughts on building plans for the attainment of a definite purpose. That leads to persistence. Organized plans, even though they may be weak and entirely impractical, encourage persistence. Given time and money, anyone can be found. If someone is paying you $175 to locate a subject, you cannot spend $350 to find someone. Practice makes perfect, and this is an exercise to fit the pieces of the puzzle to see the bigger picture.

Sting: This is a term used when you create a situation to obtain information or something. One example could be when a woman pays another woman to flirt with her boyfriend to see if he flirts back. This is a way to check if her boyfriend is a cheater or if he is faithful. If you remember the iconic film from the 1970s *The Sting*, the characters were con artists who made believe they were gamblers so that by playing poker, they could scam a mob boss out of a large amount of cash. If a con game is successful, the target does not realize he has been taken, cheated, had, duped, burnt, or played—at least not until the con men are long gone. A sting operation as it applies to law enforcement is also a deceptive operation designed to catch a person committing a crime. A typical sting will have a law-enforcement office send free tickets to a concert or a ball game, and when the subject arrives at the game, they are picked up for nonpayment of child support. One of the skip tracers' best kept secrets is mastering the different stings that are available every step you take.

Autosuggestion or self-suggestion: This is a term that applies to all suggestions and all self-administered stimuli that reach one's mind through the five senses. Some might say that it is like placing a spell on a person. The principle of autosuggestion voluntarily reaches the subconscious mind and influences it with suggestions, ideas, or thoughts. Do not confuse this with manipulation. Your ability to use autosuggestion will depend largely upon your capacity to concentrate upon a given goal until that goal becomes a burning obsession. Do not always trust your reason when carrying out your plan. Your reason can be faulty, and your reasoning ability may be lazy; if you depend on it entirely, it may disappoint you.

So go with your instinct. Follow your *hunches* and listen to that small voice from within. Use your imagination. That is the method by which this principle is operated. Remember that autosuggestion works better when emotions are expressed with feeling. When trying to induce people to give you the information that you need, use temptation to influence them. These instructions may seem abstract at first. Follow them anyway. The time will come when a whole new universe will unfold to you. Suggestion and autosuggestion are like instant persuasion, with no place to hide. Fragrance therapy is a good example of this. When we go to the supermarket, they have smells like barbecued hamburgers to make you hungry and want to buy that food right now. Buses and taxis have advertisements with pictures of delicious food that make your mouth water. They are suggestive and make us hungry at around lunchtime and dinnertime.

Operation Trust Me: Although this is not a common term like a sting, I think it is worth including a few words on an operation that the Internal Revenue Service launched many years ago. The IRS uncovered the operation after engaging in an undercover investigation code-named "Operation Trust Me." More than thirty convictions are still pending in the case, with defendants in Florida, Illinois,

New York, Ohio, and West Virginia. According to the US Attorney's office, for more than a decade, six fraudsters sold sham domestic and foreign trusts for the purpose of diverting and hiding a client's taxable income. This resulted in a $60 million tax loss to the United States, in one of the largest cases of this kind. The purpose and effect was in defrauding the government. The abusive trusts attempted to fraudulently conceal trust purchasers' true assets and income from the IRS and to illegally reduce or eliminate their income tax liability. This term in the investigative industry has now been coined and refers to locating offshore hidden assets in the form of trusts and shell corporations. New legislation has since passed and now foreign countries must disclose who the depositors are.

Follow the money trail and determine the money personality of your subject. Then use logical thinking and deductive reasoning in analyzing the paper trail. Talent, training, experience, and persistence will be assets to the fortunate few who will accumulate these financial treasures. Careful analysis of all the methods is fundamental to determine which technique is the preferred one.

Misdirection: This is the art of drawing the spectator's attention away from a secret move. This is one of the most important aspects of the art of conjuring and is a form of deception in which the attention of an audience is focused on one thing in order to distract its attention from another. It can sometimes be synonymous with distraction: the act of drawing someone's attention away from something. Remember that people are easily influenced by the opinions of others. Imagination, enthusiasm, decision, and persistence are characteristics to achieve your desire. This is a very powerful and dependable philosophy to accumulate information and other things. If you know anything about how a pickpocket works, you will know that in many cases, they will accidentally bump into you and say they are sorry. When you are distracted by the bump, they go ahead and stick their hand in your handbag or pocket to steal your wallet. The pickpockets usually find places that are crowded like elevators, escalators, or trains so they can blend into the crowd.

Tradecraft and trickcraft: These are general terms that denote a skill acquired through experience in a trade. They are also used by skip tracers as collective words for the techniques used in modern espionage. They can be used to refer to general topics or techniques, or to the specific techniques of an organization. One of the oldest tricks in the book is the honey trap. The earliest example of the honey trap can be found in the Bible, where Delilah, who seduced Samson, discovered the secret of his strength and sold it to an enemy.

It is my intention to point out some facts. There are two sides to every coin; just as the skip tracer can use these techniques and tricks, so can the fraudsters and the criminals. Step back from the circumstances and see the bigger picture. The same tools and skills are also used by your subject, just like the case of the garbologist. We all have our personal end use for the information we need to satisfy our goals and needs.

Have you ever gone into a forest and turned around and realized that you were lost and surrounded by trees? You did not know which way to go. Then someone called you, and you knew instinctively in which direction to go to get closer to that sound. You start to walk in that direction and *voila*! There is the path to the grass and your way out! As you walk away from the forest and into the gardens, you can turn around and look back and see how giganormous the forest was and how you could have been lost for days or even weeks had you taken the wrong path. When you were inside the forest, you were disoriented. Step back and see the bigger picture to function at your peak performance.

Lies, Lies, and Still More Lies

I have spoken at length about maintaining an ethical and legal approach to skip tracing, and I stand by that. However, I do want to point out that seeing the bigger picture also means making decisions about how far you go, and that you understand some basic things about human nature. The fact is we are all liars in some way or form, and we do it pretty much every day. We are all taught to lie at a very early age. When you did not do your homework in school and told the teacher, "I lost my homework, but I'll bring it in tomorrow," that is a little white lie or a pretext. Should you have told the teacher the truth—that you stayed up late watching the ball game? It is socially acceptable to tell little white lies, and it is encouraged. Another example is when someone asks you, "How do I look?" Do you say, "Good," or should you say, "You look like a clown"? The same goes when someone asks you how you are. Do you say, "Oh, I feel like crap," or do you say, "I feel fine," even if you don't.

Pretexts are sometimes synonymous with excuses; we make them up to protect someone's feelings and protect them from pain and suffering.

Little lies, and the occasional big ones, are part of workplace culture, just like boring meetings and gossipy coworkers at the watercooler. A workday that's 100 percent fib-free is rare. We're not trying to be deceptive; mostly we're trying to protect people, sometimes at our own expense. Here are five lies we're all guilty of telling: "I'd be happy to"; "No, I don't have any questions"; "My alarm didn't go off"; "I'm not sick; it's my allergies"; "I'm not behind on my schedule." So let's lighten up.

One reason you may have bought this book is because you have an interest in truth and lies. We live in a world that is constantly lying to us. Whether to sell us something—from clothes to food and beyond—or to get us to do something we normally wouldn't do. Vote for Republicans or Democrats? It's getting even harder to tell the truth from that which isn't lies, lies, and more lies. There are big lies, small lies, preposterous lies, generous lies, outrageous and hilarious lies. Some of the biggest lies are the lies we tell ourselves. Some people lie for a living, like secret agents and spies. Today's headline story is "Fake cop pulls over real cop!" Skip tracers do not need to lie to get to the bottom of the truth. Let the facts speak for themselves and don't get in the way of the facts.

Preparation is essential—but even more essential is the willingness to let go of a plan in a flash and head off in a revised direction.

—Tom Peters

Chapter 7
Real Estate Skips

*The weather-cock on the church spire,
though made of iron, would soon be broken
by the storm-wind if it did not understand
the noble art of turning to every wind.*

—Heinrich Hesse

With all the stories about all kinds of fraud in real estate, it's little wonder that a lack of trust is pervasive among sellers, buyers, and lenders. Too many people got burned during the real estate bubble. Sadly, the fraudsters are still out in force even as the housing market recovers. Some scams have dried up, so the fraudsters, crooks, and creeps just dream up new ways to rip people off.

My point here is that the skip seems to be pretty entrenched in real estate these days, presenting you with a great opportunity to find new business and to see justice done for victims at the same time. Even if you know a little something about real estate, it is important for you to get familiar with some of the scams and cons that you may encounter as you skip trace in real estate.

A Sad Case of Thievery and Suicide

A few years ago I had a case in Albany, New York, that involved a bookkeeper for a small real estate office. She was the in-house person and answered phones and took applications at the store. It appeared that over the course of the last few years, the revenues had gone down substantially and that expenses had increased. She was in charge of doing the bank reconciliation and reported back to the accountants who were not in-house. The private investigator handling the case said that funds had gone missing from the corporate bank accounts, and they needed to know if the funds were going into the bookkeeper's personal account, because they were sure that she was stealing money from the company.

As it turned out, she was embezzling money, but not that much in the form of checks written to her from the company. But she was laundering money on her American Express and then paying the American Express bill from the company bank account. This totaled huge sums because she loved going with her daughter to gamble at the casinos and then shop till she dropped. By the time the case had gotten to me, the bookkeeper already knew that her employer was up to something because they had been asking for the American Express statements. The second day that I was working on the case, I got a call from my client, the private investigator, telling me to cease all work because the bookkeeper had taken her own life. I asked how she had committed suicide, but in order to protect the privacy of the family they did not want to anyone to know. This is why this topic is so important to the skip tracer.

Real estate fraud is rampant in our society and a major contributor to the real estate bubble bursting. Title fraud is the illegal transfer of property to another party or entity in order to defer, hinder, or defraud creditors and lenders. Title fraud is a deception made for personal gain. It is an intentional misrepresentation, concealment, or omission of material facts, done with the purpose of deceiving another which causes detriment to them. The perpetrator often targets both lenders and individuals and has premeditated the crime. It is also known as a "slander on title."

In Real Estate, Skips Abound and It's up to Skip Tracers to Track Them Down

In a broad sense, a fraud is an intentional deception made for personal gain or to damage another. *Title* is a term for a bundle of rights in a piece of property where a party may own either a legal interest or an equitable interest. The rights in the bundle may be broken up and held by different parties. This is also a formal document that serves as proof of ownership.

The process of transferring an interest in real estate from one party to another is a conveyance. A conveyance of document is required in order to transfer ownership in a property to another person or entity. Title is distinct from possession, a right that often accompanies ownership but is not sufficient to prove it. Sometimes, both possession and title may be transferred independently of each other.

The legal instrument used to transfer title is the deed. The famous rule is that a "thief cannot convey good title." Title searches are routine and mandatory in most states for purchase of real estate. Nationwide a standard title search, generally accompanied by title insurance, is required under the law as a part of ownership transfer.

Title Fraud Is Uncommon in Real Estate, but When It's Done, the Skips Are Clever about Circumventing the Law

Title fraud refers to the processes required to transfer ownership of real estate with a fraudulent conveyance. The preparation, execution, verification, and lodgment of various legal documents are important elements of a fraudulent conveyance. The intentional transfer of assets, immediately prior to and in anticipation of, less than adequate consideration is intended to place assets out of reach of rightful creditors. So title fraud is the illegal transfer of property to another party or entity in order to defer, hinder, or defraud creditors.

The equitable title refers to the actual enjoyment and use of a property, whereas a legal title implies actual ownership. An example is a trust. In a trust, one person may own the legal title, such as the trustees. Another may own the equitable title such as the beneficiary. This type of fraud—like mortgage, insurance, or foreclosure fraud—is made up of simultaneous frauds. This involves a knowing misrepresentation or misleading statement, and this is the crime of title fraud.

Potential fraudulent information in title commitments is the easiest way to follow the paper trail. A title commitment is a written report by a title insurance company setting forth the conditions under which it will insure a particular property, showing all current claims against the property before a sale or loan transaction. The title commitment would usually be written and signed by a title insurance agent of the title insurance company. The title commitment reflects the condition of the title to the home. It tells the buyer whether the taxes and assessments are paid and if the property is encumbered. The fraudster is not the smartest person on the planet, so try to figure out if they made stupid or immature mistakes.

A Good Skip Tracer Can Trip Up a Title Fraudster Simply by Watching for Stupid Mistakes

In the majority of my work, I see that the fraudster is the skip that my client is looking for. Once I can identify what they are doing and report that to the client, then my client can decide what action they want to take. My job is to report the facts and not taint the information. Sometimes just by approaching the skip and letting the fraudster know that you know what they are doing is criminal will bring your skip to the table to offer a settlement as a sign of goodwill. It is another tool in your toolbox or another secret for your bag of tricks.

Title insurance can benefit either the payer or the payee, should the beneficiary suffer any damages due to clouded or false title, or forgery! Title insurance compensates the damaged party to the extent of the damages. Forged documents are manipulated using techniques similar to check washing. This process involves using a chemical mix to wash the ink off of the check and then you get a blank check to fill out as you wish. Sometimes they will create a template for certain items to be forged and fill in the blanks. Templates are reused. One example of this would be a mortgage application that they fill out with make-believe information. An insurance policy that insures a party against loss due to a defective title is one instrument that gets manipulated. The insurance companies and banks become victims of fraud. It is hard to tell the difference when you are relying on the expertise of counsel who is also being duped by the criminals. In the end, we all end up paying for this.

Fraudsters have extremely sophisticated methods of manipulating data. Some have tax returns on computer programs that are cooked in order to meet the requirements of the lenders. Whatever ratios the credit extension underwriters will require can be met. Their expectations are never too high. The criminals make believe they are preparing a real tax return, W-2, 1099, or whatever will be required can be created and is never a problem. Wishful thinking and technology get them through their days, all at the click of a mouse.

Mortgage Fraud Is Another Hot Area for Real Estate Skips, Making It a Great Possibility for Your Skip Tracing Company

A mortgage is a simple written instrument that creates a lien by pledging real property as collateral security for a debt. These liens can be manipulated using various methods like data manipulation. Debt instruments are basic future payments or series of payments, or a debt that one party owes to another party. They are also known as income streams or cash flow instruments. These can be manipulated at many levels. Light your creativity on fire and let your ideas out. These high-end crooks have a taste for the good life at our expense.

Fraudsters and House Flipping Are Another Major Area of Skips in Real Estate

Every investigator seeking the truth needs to understand fraud in flipping. Flipping can be a criminal scheme. Fraud in flipping is a fraud-for-profit scheme where recently acquired property is resold for a profit with an artificially inflated value. The property is resold within a short time frame, often after making only superficial improvements. Fraud in flipping often involves collusion between a real estate appraiser, a mortgage originator, and a closing agent—and your skip could be one of the players. I have seen this in my own practice.

The cooperation of a real estate appraiser is necessary since a false and artificially inflated appraisal report is required. This is also referred to as collusion. The buyer who is also the ultimate borrower may or may not be aware of the situation. This type of fraud is one of the most costly for lenders because the loss is always substantial. Fraud examiners are like money in your pocket. Watch out for the flippers. Recent changes in the way appraisers are assigned properties to appraise has greatly diminished the fraud on the appraisal side (appraisers are drawn from a blind pool, meaning they can't be manipulated in advance). But fraudsters are still out there.

Professional real estate investors cash in on foreclosed properties by buying in bulk and reselling at a profit. They will buy a house for $1.3 million and pay only $486,000 in cash, and then resell that home for $800,000, making a profit of $314,000. Regulations for *professional* real estate developers and real estate agents dictate that you cannot go inside the home to inspect it. You can only look at it from the outside, so that equals a huge risk because these are mostly cash deals. These regulations are for bulk sales only. Seek and you will find.

Understanding who is a target of potential fraud is important information that needs to be uncovered. This applies most importantly to the skip tracer because your deadbeat could be picking his targets, and you need to figure out what pool of victims is he targeting. Any person who is looking to buy or sell a property is a potential victim of fraud. Lenders are victims of fraud because they become the prey. Insurance companies are victims of fraud. Municipalities are victims because they are cheated out of tax flow from the real estate. Neighborhoods are victims because when fraud occurs, it hurts everyone at the global level. Real estate fraud is a contributor to the global economic crises due to the major losses of everyone. How much is your share of the bill?

Some targets of potential fraud are mortgage lenders, attorneys, real estate agents, brokers, insurers, insurance agents, paralegals, and other real estate industry professionals, borrowers/lenders, sellers/buyers, and our economy and society as a whole because of the trickle-down theory. Many agents lack the professional skills needed to fulfill the legal duty and to act in the best interest of consumers and lenders. Licensing standards are determined by individual states, as are continuing education requirements.

Robo-Signing Foreclosure Documents Represents a Fraud against Homeowners, and in Many Cases the Bank Is the Skip

Robo-signing is when an employee of a mortgage servicing company signs foreclosure documents without reviewing them. Rather than actually reviewing the individual details of each case, robo-signers assume the paperwork to be correct and sign it automatically, like robots.

In the third and fourth quarters of 2010, a robo-signing scandal emerged in the United States involving mortgage companies and a number of major US banks. Robo-signing comes from the association of this robotic process of the mass production of false statements. Banks had to halt thousands of foreclosures in numerous states when it became known that the paperwork was illegitimate because the signers had not actually reviewed it. While some robo-signers were middle managers, others were temporary workers with virtually no understanding of the work they were doing, and there were also those insiders with a vested interest. The robo-signing scandal was an opportunity for homeowners to challenge foreclosures in court, negotiate with lenders, and buy time. We have all become victims of this.

If You Are a Victim of Robo-Signing, There Are Several Things You Can Do

There are several things you can do if you are a victim of mortgage fraud in the form of a robo-signer. If you are a skip tracer investigating a particular deadbeat that is a perpetrator, you need to understand how the process works and how to stay ahead of the criminals. The mortgage fraud market is a big user of skip tracing services. In order to be able to service that market, we must be able to comprehend the ins and outs of how these frauds are committed. If your skip is a participant in any fraud, you must be able to detect which fraud is which, otherwise you will be looking in the wrong place and won't find what you are looking for. If he is a robo-signer and you are concentrating on the flippers, that will lead you to a dead end. You should investigate having a forensic audit and a securitization audit performed on your mortgage. These audits will examine your loan and determine if the bank has overcharged you, given you an interest rate that is much higher than it ought to be, or if you are a victim of a robo-signer or other mortgage fraud. Foreclosure-gate is an unresolved issue that is causing fear in America. Always think like a fraudster.

Many industry insiders or mortgage brokers have been known to have criminal records and were out preying on innocent victims and making big bucks off of the banks. The cost of this loss is passed on to all of us in one way or another. Where are the regulators when you need them? From one insider to another insider, who's the outsider?

As a Skip Tracer, You Should Always Respond to Any Red Flags You Encounter during Any Transaction, Especially One Involving Real Estate

Some transactional red flags to watch for are these high-level flags that need our attention:

- Social Security number discrepancies within the loan file

- address discrepancies within the loan file

- verifications addressed to a specific party's attention

- verifications completed on the same day they were ordered

- verifications completed on weekend or holiday

- documentation includes deletions, correction fluid, or other alteration

- numbers on the documentation appear to be *squeezed* due to alteration and different handwriting or font type and styles within

Red flags in the mortgage application to watch for include the following:

- significant or contradictory changes from handwritten to a typed application

- unsigned or undated application

- employer's address shown only as a post office box

- loan purpose is cash-out refinance on a recently acquired property

- buyer currently resides in subject property

- same telephone number for applicant and employer

- extreme payment shock may indicate inflated income

- purchaser of investment property doesn't own residence

If the sales contract contains any of these red flags, stop and investigate them thoroughly.

- Arms-length transaction: the seller is real estate broker, relative, employer, etc.

- The seller is not currently reflected on title.

- The purchaser is not the applicant.

- Purchasers were deleted from/added to sales contract.

- No real estate agent is involved.

- A power of attorney is used.

- A second mortgage is indicated, but not disclosed on the application.

- Earnest money deposit equals the entire down payment, or is an odd amount.

- Multiple deposit checks have inconsistent dates; for example, check #303 is dated 10/1 and check #299 is dated 11/1, or checks are out of sequence.

- Name and/or address on earnest money deposit check differs from the buyer.

- The real estate commission is excessive.

- The contract is dated after credit documents.

- The contract is a "boiler plate" with limited fill-in-the-blank terms, not reflective of a true negotiation.

Low pricing means lowering the price of the transaction to make it more enticing to the buyer. Pricing in economics and business is the result of an exchange and from that trade we assign a numerical monetary value to a good, service, or asset. Low pricing then means to underprice the value of what must be given up by one party, the buyer, in order to obtain something offered by another party. Price means different things to different participants in an exchange because of the market and the elasticity of the supply and demand curve.

Price theory asserts that the market price reflects interaction between two opposing considerations. In real estate fraud, this does not apply nor does any other theory or principle. They write the rules they play by. Beware of low pricing schemes that are too good to be true. They are usually just plain scams conducted by some savvy scammers. It is the skip tracer's role to detect this.

Last-minute and delayed loan packages can also signal red flags to look for. Signing a lock-in agreement with one set of terms can result in a mortgage bank coming back and changing the pricing and terms of a mortgage before the closing, costing more. Lenders, brokers, and banks routinely change loan terms between the time of application and closing. Sometimes they have legitimate reasons for doing so. Lenders, banks, and brokers promise to make loans on one set of terms, then change those terms before closing, pointing out their promises came with conditions. Lenders perform a preliminary credit review, but usually don't thoroughly check the other information borrowers provide. They then issue so-called *conditional approvals* which say something along the lines of "We'll loan you X dollars at Y rate and points." Some customers *lock in* those terms by signing rate lock agreements. Overcome your obstacles to success.

No loan, no matter what you apply for, is guaranteed. It's all about the findings of the loan as the process goes on. There are variables during the process that may change the initial assumed profile of the loan. Things can change the price of the loan, and delayed loan packages with last-minute changes leave lots of room for errors that are intentional and nonintentional.

Straw buyers are loan applicants used by fraud perpetrators to obtain mortgages, and are used to disguise the true buyer or the true nature of the transaction. Mortgage payments are made by an entity other than the borrower. The loan is usually an early payment default, and usually a first-time home buyer, with a substantial increase in housing expense or a buyer who does not intend to occupy because of an unrealistic commute, the size or condition of property, etc. No real estate agent is employed, which is a non-arms-length transaction. Power of attorney may be used. It could be a *boiler plate* contract with limited insertions, not reflective of a true negotiation or income; savings and/or credit patterns are inconsistent with applicant's overall profile; high LTV (loan to value), limited reserves, and/or seller-paid. These straw buyer examples are red flags, and skip tracers need to pay special attention here.

An *air loan* is a loan to a straw or nonexistent buyer, on a nonexistent property. Air loans typically involve straw buyers, so refer to straw buyer red flags. No real estate agent is employed. Mortgage payments are made by an entity other than the borrower or common payer among multiple loans or a common mailing address among multiple loans, or you are unable to independently validate the chain of title. The lender may be experiencing financial distress—another red flag for the skip tracer to concentrate on. Your skip could be the victim or the perpetrator in any of these fraud schemes, so make sure that every step is covered since often times these criminals work in gangs and run it like a legitimate business. You might actually need to sting them by setting them up. You might go in and make believe you are a potential buyer in order to see what the actual process involves so that you can figure out the rest. That is also a form of competitive intelligence.

A *double sale* is the sale of one mortgage note to more than one investor. Mortgage payments are made by an entity other than the borrower or the mailing address is not the borrower's address or two mortgages are recorded on the same property or the mortgage is not recorded in first lien position. These are more signs of red flags for the researcher to investigate.

Other irregularities and red flags include a Social Security number that was issued recently, or a death claim filed under a Social Security number; income and assets are frequently misrepresented; employment and/or addresses on a credit report do not match the borrower's; A *Mickey Mouse payee* is when a fictitious payee is set up on a company's payroll records in order to commit fraud. Make sure when verifying salary data that the name and Social Security number match the information on the application. This is one of the most difficult frauds to pick up because it requires insiders, and they are intent on deceiving you right from the start by concealing the true nature of the transaction. This form of money laundering is a real living and the antifraud community is ready to step up to the plate and detect the existence, nature, source, ownership, and disposition of property derived from criminal activity. These are also a form of embezzlement. Examine this under a microscope.

Accounting anomalies that investigators look for are the secrets to success. Accountants not only must understand how to interpret the law, they must know how to account for it. Due diligence is part of what investigators search for. Most companies, whether they use cash or accrual basis accounting, adhere to GAPP—generally accepted accounting principles. Not using GAPP is a red flag to watch out for. It means a departure from the normal and warrants additional attention because that can be where the crime occurred.

Padding *short sales* is another common scam. Short sales are two loans on one property, usually a mortgage and a piggyback loan. A second lender can block the short sale of a property unless his security interest is satisfied. Sometimes these criminals seek cash on the side, and they want that fact omitted and do not disclose it in the settlement statement. This is also known as a kickback, and it is a red flag and a violation of the law. Loan modifications are prime targets for this type of crime. With one in every five properties in foreclosure and over one hundred thousand loan modifications, the odds for committing real estate fraud are increasing at an astounding rate. Knowing this fact will help everyone in cutting fraud and slashing waste from the system.

A *cash scam* is when you go on vacation and see a property that you plan to buy. You make an offer and settle for a price. The owner of the house signs a deed. Since you are away, you plan to pay the owner by a home equity line of credit. He won't accept that and insists that you pay cash—which you agree to. After a couple of days, when you apply for a loan to improve your home, you are unable to do so as you find out that the "owner" was not the actual owner, and there is a dispute in the title.

The *forged title scam* is a common fraud. A forged title can be used to get a loan for a property that the scammer does not own. A deed has the forged signatures of a thief. The forged deed is authenticated. Once the document has been notarized, the same document is used as collateral for applying for a loan. Alternatively, the document can also be used to inflate the value of the property by unfair means and is finally sold off to a buyer. Both ways, the thief is benefited. The fraudsters have careers to pursue.

This is the *vacant property scam* where the fraudster uses unoccupied buildings in a scam to make money on the properties by selling them. The perpetrator allegedly transfers vacant properties to himself and then sells them. He files bogus mortgage records with the city stating it was collateral for a fictitious loan from a construction company he owned, so that no one else could claim the property. Get to the nitty-gritty of the problem.

On May 20, 2009, President Obama signed into law the Fraud Enforcement and Recovery Act of 2009, providing additional funding for fighting fraud. Additional legislation was introduced which made it a crime to make a materially false statement or to willfully, overvalue a property in order to influence any action by a mortgage lending business. Currently, these false statement offences only apply to federal agencies, banks, and credit associations, and do not necessarily extend to private mortgage lending businesses, even if they are handling federally-regulated or federally-insured mortgages. Similar to expanding the definition of *financial institution*, this provision would ensure that private mortgage brokers and companies are held fully accountable under this federal fraud provision. This is particularly important as false appraisal fraud has proliferated during the recent global financial crisis.

Steps you should take if you suspect fraud are to file a police report at your local precinct where the crime occurred. Contact the three consumer reporting agencies and submit a consumer statement to your credit report. Use the resources provided in this book. Look at things upside down, upside down backward and forward, and tear the issues apart. Real estate fraud requires a great deal of planning and coordination among numerous insiders; it takes a team to pull it off and it takes us as a team to fight back. What is truth is truth and what is not true is not true, and that is the end of a road.

Skip Tracers Must Always Consider the Value of Real Property as Potentially Hidden Assets

A discussion about real estate fraud and the skip tracer's role in tracking down the real estate fraudsters would not be complete without emphasizing that the hidden asset issue is just as important. People hide money in real property, and it's up to the skip tracer to find it.

Any skip tracer who does not thoroughly search through the gold mines of information tucked away in real estate transactions is missing valuable information that can help you collect money for your client using skip tracing. Residents and business owners unite to wrestle with the question of how neighborhoods can encourage development while keeping the qualities residents cherish. Big cities are no different. Real property owners can live anywhere. Wherever there is property owned, there are usually lots of other hidden assets including bank accounts and other goodies. This also applies to industrial; commercial, and office properties. Researching property records on residential, commercial, land, and all other types of real estate properties in the United States including water rights and air rights is required research.

Real properties sometimes contain silos of commodities that have values that change from moment to moment based on market conditions. These are assets that need to be extracted from the ground, in most cases. These natural resources are things like forests that get cut down and then sold off for cash. The using up of natural resources is known as *depletion*. Other assets that are depleted are petroleum, oil, gas wells, metals, water, mines, minerals, quarrying stone, geothermal deposits, and capitalized costs. These assets are located on real property.

Entities that meet the definition of having an economic interest in a property are eligible to claim deductions for *depletion*. For accounting and financial reporting purposes, depletion is meant to assist in accurately identifying the value of the assets. There are two types of depletion. Cost depletion is calculated by taking the property's total recoverable units and number of units sold into account. Percentage depletion looks at the property's gross income and taxable income limit. This is the accounting method that follows the paper trail. This tool allows the skip tracer to physically see and understand how the hidden assets are transferred. Everything only changes form.

Here are more terms you should keep in mind:

Equity: This can mean you own your own home and have a financial stake in it. Or it can mean that you hold an ownership interest in a corporation in the form of common stock or preferred stock. It also refers to total assets minus total liabilities, in which case it is also referred to as shareholder's equity or net worth or book value. In real estate, it is the difference between what a property is worth and what the owner owes against that property—for example, the difference between the house value and the remaining mortgage or loan payments on a house. In the context of a futures trading account, it is the value of the securities in the account, assuming that the account is liquidated at the going price. In the context of a brokerage account, it is the net value of the account or the value of securities in the account less any margin requirements. Any way you look at it, there is plenty of equity. Times are tough and credit is hard to get, so look at the small details.

Hidden assets: These are assets that may be undervalued or not stated on a financial statement. Hidden assets can be in the form of patents, trademarks, copyrights, intellectual property, air miles, or undervalued real estate. Investors who are value-oriented will often try to identify a company's hidden values. These are not shown on the financial statement because they are too difficult to quantify. The best you can do is to approximate them on the day that you are preparing the statements. Because these assets cannot be immediately found on the balance sheet does not mean they don't have a huge value. Make sure to analyze these assets carefully while building your own hidden assets. Take the time to study the results and put everything together in the right format. Recognize that you are adding to your own net worth, not just financially but in self-growth. You are growing as a person due to the knowledge you have gained as a process of doing the work and practicing. This experience in personal growth is particularly valuable for skip tracers. It is also valuable for anyone who wants to grow, as with most concepts in this book.

Real estate represents a lucrative market for skip tracers because there is still a lot of fraudulent activity going on out there, and people need our help. Real estate also represents a literal treasure trove of hidden assets we can track down when it comes to collecting money to settle judgments for our clients. As a skip tracer, you'll no doubt work in this market segment, and I think you'll find it exciting. There's a lot happening every day!

Wealth is the product of a man's capacity to think.

—Ayn Rand

Chapter 8
Internet Search Strategies

An ounce of wisdom is worth more than tons of cleverness.

—*Baltasar Gracian*

The Internet is ubiquitous. It lives in practically every aspect of our lives. In fact, it is almost impossible to escape from it, and billions of us are just fine with that. As such a powerful source of information and communication in the daily lives of people throughout the world, it's no small wonder that the Internet has become one of the most powerful weapons in the skip tracer's arsenal. We use the Internet for every case. I can't even imagine what my job would be like without it.

So, we need to take a good hard look at how we can use the Internet to find deadbeats, scammers, and unintentional skips. The online databases that house vast troves of public and closed-source records are major resources. Search engines can reap excellent results, if you know how to use them. Social media is a veritable gold mine. It always amazes me how much data people put up on the web. Skips don't seem to get it. We go straight to Facebook and Twitter as a matter of course, and we often find a skip chirping about like a little bird in a cage when he or she has done everything else imaginable to hide. Go figure!

The following chapter will show you how I use the Internet to track down skips. After that, I've provided you with a wealth of potential knowledge in chapter 9, where you'll find hundreds of links you can access during your intelligence gathering efforts. Let's start out with the basics of the Internet and go from there.

Internet Searches Are a Fast and Often Easy Way to Get Ahead on the Skip

Many search on the Internet to find restaurants, stores, movies and entertainment, and things we use in our everyday lives. We use maps to see how to get to where we are going and then see what cool activities are in that town to enjoy. Learning search strategies early in the game can prevent frustration down the road. Let the purpose of your search determine the search to be used. You can search for images, sounds, videos, news, résumés, media 3-D models and colors, and file types. You can use the "find" key by hitting CTRL and the letter *F*, at the same time, to search on a particular page or in a document. You can limit your search within a time frame. You can also limit your search to a range of anything you want. Remember to look at the related searches on the bottom of the page when you are searching.

Think about the conceptual space (the ideas surrounding your search) and go from the vague to the explicit and specific. You can do this by using the "define" feature in Google or the search engine you are using. To focus on your query, put yourself into the mind-set of the subject and look around a little bit. Use generic words and synonyms to do your search. Every word matters. For example try these: "blue sky" versus "sky blue" or "brittney" versus "brittany" versus "britteny." You will get entirely different results. Capitalizations do not matter. We will discuss other operators to filter our results like double quotes, adding results using the plus sign (+) and removing results with the minus (-) sign later on. These advanced techniques are the best time savers. Rather than search manually, you can use a command to filter what is waste.

Variant data is information that changes. One example of this would be the circumference of the earth. It varies depending on how we measure it. If we measure at the equator, it will give us one size, but if it is measured higher up, we will get a smaller number. To verify data or a quote or something else, we can use the "Advanced Search" icon and search further in that. We can also run our mouse over the arrows to the right of the search results to see a small thumbnail of the website so that we don't have to waste time by clicking on the link and going to the website. It will give you a preview of each result in your search.

The Internet has every tool you will need to find what you need. You have a screwdriver (your computer), but you think you need a hammer. Learn to use the screwdriver, because that is all that you need. You have all the tools at your fingertips, so concentrate on perfecting your technique and learn how to use them effectively.

Searching like a pro is easy if we learn the basics. Once we understand those, we can build on those platforms. One of the basic building blocks is understanding the difference between a search engine and a directory.

Search engine: This is a program that searches websites for specific keywords and returns a list of the sites where the keywords were found; one example is http://www.google.com.

Web directory: This is like a search engine, but it will narrow your search criteria even further by geographic area, business, industry, interest, or other variables you select; one example is http://directory.google.com.

Knowing how search engines work will help us set up our search criteria to obtain better results. When we query a search engine to find information, it must search through hundreds of millions of web pages. In order to do that, it uses software robots called *spiders* to list the words we are looking for. The spider builds this list by a process called web crawling, which scans the content of the web page for keywords or *meta tags* that are significant in locating that page. Different search engines use different methods of indexing the information, but they all use an algorithm, which is just a simple procedure for determining the relevance of the information in the index to what the user is searching for.

Boolean Logic May Sound Alien to You at First, but Knowing What It Is and How to Use It Will Earn You Big Bucks as a Skip Tracer

Understanding Boolean logic is the key to effective searching on the Internet and the best search strategy for finding complex search expressions. Boolean logic is symbolic logic developed by George Boole, a British mathematician, in the 1800s. Boolean logic refers to the logical relationship among search terms, and much database searching is based on the principles of Boolean logic. For our purposes, think of it as a form of algebra that consists most importantly three logical operators. Each operator can be visually described by using Venn diagrams, as shown below.

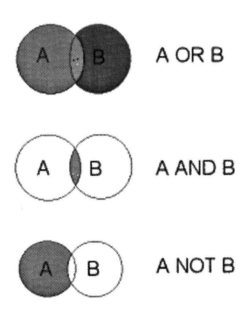

A OR B

A AND B

A NOT B

Using Boolean logic in Google or any search engine is easy. By default, Google puts an "AND" in between each word in your search criteria, giving you the intersection of all the terms. Based on a search criteria of A = rain, and B = snow; A not B; A or B, we will see how to use these variables to narrow or expand our search. Searching for "rain snow" will give you all results with both words on the page. Searching for "rain OR snow" will return all pages with either of the words on it. Searching for "rain–snow" will return pages with the word *rain*, but not pages with the word *snow* on them. Google normally will not search for common words like *to*, *the*, *I*, *and*, *of*, *from*, etc. But you can force Google to include these terms in your search by prefixing them with the "+" symbol.

Another standard is the requirement to search for phrases within quotations, "snow rain." When you enter more than one word in a search engine, the space between the words has a logical meaning that directly affects your results. This is known as the default syntax. You will get back documents that contain both the words *rain* and *snow*. This is because the space between the words defaults to the Boolean *and*. Most search tools nowadays default to *and* logic.

Before you select a search tool, always think about your topic and what you are trying to find. Keep in mind that search engines do not index all the documents available on the web.

Taking the Time to Learn How to Power-Search with Google Can Reap Great Rewards

Google Search makes it amazingly easy to find information. Learn about the powerful advanced tools they provide to help you find just the right information when the stakes are high. Power-searching with Google is a free online, community-based course showcasing search techniques and how to use them to solve real, everyday problems. These classes provide interactive activities to practice new skills. They also have opportunities to connect with others using Google Groups, Google+, and Hangouts on Air. I attended these webinars, and I recommend them to any tracer who wants to understand the finer points of skip tracing. I would say that every skip tracer should attend these classes as part of their training as a researcher. This is a valuable tool and a first step to getting better at what you are doing.

Google's latest move into social media is Google+ which is the largest growing social site online. Google+ has once again brought some new tools to the digital table. One of my favorites is Hangouts. Google describes Hangouts as a "front porch." Someone can drop in and say hi just like anyone could drop by when you're on your porch or at home. Google+ Hangouts can help you do the interacting right from your desk.

Google+ Hangouts On Air is a free and easy solution to reach people via videos. Hangouts will allow you to video chat with up to 9 different people at once. Hangouts On Air allows you to publicly broadcast your Hangouts on YouTube and your Google+ stream for anyone to watch. It's like having access to your own live video show on the web—viewable to anyone in the world. You can also share your screen and slides.

Become a power searcher and learn to solve real, everyday problems using advanced search features. Check out the G+ Insider's Guide for the latest news, tips, and tricks on Google+. Not all networks are created equal; each comes with its own specific benefits, features, and uses. And some are more equal than others.

Google Glass or Google Glasses are the computerized glasses that will be released next year to the public. They are now as light as regular sunglasses, come with a touch panel on the side, a button on top to take photos and videos, and a transparent screen to show information. They perch just above a person's regular vision so they don't interfere with ordinary eye contact. Google believes they're better for capturing a first-person view of the world, such as spontaneous photographs people would miss if they had to take time to dig out a camera.

Advanced Searches on Google Are Easy and Fast

Google operators are query words or symbols that perform special actions when searching. Here are the advanced search operators you can use when searching in Google by entering the following operator in the box at the top of any Google page, and clicking the "search" button:

Here are some examples from the growing list of popular symbols that are supported:

- plus sign (+) to search for things like blood type [AB+] or the programming language [C++]

- "at" sign (@) for finding social tags like [@google] or [@ladygaga]

- ampersand (&) for strongly connected ideas and phrases like [A&E] or [Brothers & Sisters]

- dollar sign ($) to indicate prices: so [canon 400] and [canon $400] give different results

- hashtag or number sign (#) to search for trending topics indicated by hashtags like [#lifewithoutgoogle]

- dash (-) will sometimes be used as a sign that the words around it are very strongly connected, as in [twelve-year-old dog] and [cross-reference]

- underscore symbol (_) is not ignored when it connects two words, like [quick_sort]

- tilde sign (~) immediately in front of a word to search for that word as well as its synonyms: [~food facts] includes results for "nutrition facts"

- quotation marks around words ["9(any word)"] to search for an exact phrase in an exact order. Keep in mind that searching with quotes might exclude relevant results. For instance, a search for "Alexander Bell" will miss pages that refer to "Alexander G. Bell".

Search for specific types of files—such as PDF, PPT, or XLS—by adding "filetype" and the three-letter file abbreviation [affordable health care act filetype:ppt].

Use Advanced Image Search to find an exact size, color, or type of photo or drawing. With the tools in the left panel, you can filter your search to include only photos with faces, clip art, high-res images, and more. Try searching "mount hood".

Google's spell checker automatically defaults to the most common spelling of a given word, whether or not you spell it correctly.

Always Remember to Expand Your Parameters When Searching on the Internet

Narrowing or expanding a search is as easy as using "wildcards." One widely used wildcard is the asterisk (*). To expand your search on the name "Al" we would type into the search bar Al*; that would return Alexander, Alexandra, Alexis, Alana, Alma, Albert, Alberto, Alberta, Alfred, Alfredo, Alfreda, Aldo, Alice, Allison, Alfonso, and Allen. This will return many more hits than by narrowing your search. To narrow your search, type the name into the search bar using quotation marks "Alphonse." This will return exact matches and fewer hits.

Use other Google operators like Joseph William + city, state. Also try Joey William + zip code. Search for Joe William in city, state or query Joe William in zip code. If the subject is really William Joseph, then look for Billy, Bill, Willie, Will, Willy + city, state or zip code.

Variations on spelling of names can mean the difference between finding the right person or the wrong person. Consider different options to search the same criteria. *Clement* can be spelled out as: Klement, Clemente, Clemens, Kiement, Kiemens, Clementhius, Clemmie, Clementine, Clemence, Clementhia, Clementina, or Clemmy. This one could be male or female.

Reversing the order of the first name and last name can mean finding the wrong person. These are just a few examples of how we could slip up: Paul Mitchell or Mitchell Paul, Mark Anthony or Anthony Mark, James Russell or Russell James, Kristine Christian or Christian Kristine, Ahmed Mohammed or Mohammed Ahmed, Kim Lee or Lee Kim. Using quotation marks will help with this situation.

Confusing male and female names can mean looking for the wrong person. Gender can send us searching in the wrong direction. Examples of unisex names are Chris, Terry, Carrol, Lesley, Michelle, Meridith, Bobby, Toni, Ariel, Dana, and Jesse. Make sure to double-check your source.

Nicknames can become so sophisticated that we need to clarify who our target is. Kitty is a derivative of Katherine, Katharine, Catherine, Catharine, Kathy, Cathy,

Kathryn, Katheryn, Kathie, Kathleen, Katerina, Kathye, Katie, Kathe, Kathi, Kittie, Kitti, Kit, Kat, Kaya, Kate, Katey, Cathleen, Cathi, Cathe, Cathie, Cathey, and Catie.

The correct spelling of the proper name will be important. Margaret, Margret, Margarete, Marguerette, Margarethe, Margit, and Marguerite are variations of this name.

Names like Kim Lee versus Lee Kim can be two entirely different people. One can be a Chinese female and the latter a male Korean. If we are looking at other alternate names like Kimberly, Kimmie, or Kimmy, it might be harder to identify the right subject. That's why it's so important to start out with the correct spelling of the subject's name, if at all possible. You'll save lots of time that way, and that's always a good thing.

Latin names or names with prefixes such as Mac, Mc, El, Al, or Il can also be tricky to solve. Consider these: DeRosario, DaRosairo, DiRosairo, D'Rosario, DelRosairo, DolRosairo, DelRoseirio, DilRosaro, and DilRosaios. The variations can seem endless. Other nationalities can be just as complex and can be, as they say in the sport or art, just as difficult to hunt!

Other names that have so many variations will get tricky. If you are looking for Anthony Marc but your subject goes by Tony, you will need to ask for him or her in the right way, otherwise he will never be in when you call. Same thing goes for other common names that have very specific nicknames. Think about Richar, Richard, Ricard, Ricardo, Richardo, Richi, Richie, Richy, Ricky, Ricki,

Rickie, Dick, Dicky, Dickie, Rich. Then there is Joseph, Yusef, Yosef, Joe, Joey … and I hope I made my point.

Believe It or Not, There's an "Invisible" Web Skip Tracers Can Use to Track Down Their Subjects

Comprehending and discovering the invisible web will expand your knowledge base and improve your performance. The invisible web is also known as the deep web. The term refers mainly to web pages that cannot be indexed by a regular search engine, rendering the data "invisible" to the user. One of the most common reasons that a website's content is not indexed is because of the site's use of dynamics, which opens a portal for potential spider traps. Web pages can also fall into the invisible web if there are no links leading to them, since spiders typically harvest through links that lead them from one location to another. Data on the invisible web is not inaccessible. The information is stored on a computer server and can be accessed using a browser; the data must be found using means other than the regular search engines, such as Google.

How does the invisible web differ from the visible web? The visible or surface web is accessible to the traditional search engines. The invisible or deep web is in a constant state of change and is made up of hundreds of thousands of publicly accessible databases and is much bigger than the visible web. Because the Internet is a dynamic medium, it changes every second, so something that you saw on a site yesterday may no longer be there, because it was changed in some shape or form. Let's say that you needed to find an article in yesterday's news or a photo that was once present but has been taken down. You can try Google's "cache" results, which is a snapshot of the site when it was indexed for their server, but it will not provide the date, or we can search the publicly accessible invisible web.

Finding invisible web documents is easy. Several directories for invisible websites are as follows:

http://www.specialissues.com/ is a solution for tracking and finding industrial and trade magazine special issues. Specialissues.com is an online database of editorial calendars, special issues, and content "mined" from trade and industrial magazine websites.

http://www.scirus.com/srsapp/ Scirus is the most comprehensive scientific research tool on the web. With over 450 million scientific items indexed at last count, it allows researchers to search for not only journal content but also scientists' home pages, courseware, preprint server material, patents and institutional repository, and website information.

http://lii.org/ Librarians' Internet Index (LII) is a publicly funded website and weekly newsletter serving California, the nation, and the world. You can search and browse this website for the best of the web. It has over twenty thousand entries, also maintained by the librarians, organized into fourteen main topics and nearly three hundred related topics.

http://library.albany.edu/subject/ University Library at the University at Albany has links to outside journals and departmental databases.

http://www.archive.org/ Old web pages get indexed, and locating them is as simple as knowing where to look for them. If you have a website you want to search for, then you may want to start out by going to the "WayBack Machine." After you run your initial search, you can compare the archives and then compare the dates against each other. Use the comparison tool to save time. Use the "Advanced Feature" to search by year. The asterisks next to the date will tell us when WayBack noticed the changes. Supercool search tool.

Tracking on the Internet Goes Both Ways

The term *cyber tracking* means you're being tracked over multiple different websites, effectively following you as you browse the web. They use either cookies, or hard-to-delete "supercookies," or other means, to link their records of each new page they see you visit to their records of all the pages you've visited in the previous minutes, months, and years. Skip tracers can use the same exact products that businesses use. This is one step in these step-by-step guidelines that cannot be overlooked. Cyber tracking is one of the skip tracer's best-kept secrets.

There is software available to track animals, birds, insects, and even sexual predators. There is also software for tracing cyber attacks and cyber predators. Some are cyber crimes and some are just innovative techniques. The purpose is to gather information, track online purchases, or track voices—track whatever. Almost everything is traceable now.

As cyber technology begins to grow and new advancements develop, what was once just a fantasy becomes a reality. There are apps similar to Global Positioning Systems (GPS) that provide full real-time map-based tracking of all vehicles, just like UPS tracks packages. Some other software packages offer mutations or hybrid combinations of these online tracking methods. With the national gas price crises, there are "gas apps" available for tracking gas prices.

Many of these apps are converting to a "chip & pin" system to be able to deter criminals from stealing and committing fraud. These have features that are similar to the swipe cards. Some new computers come preloaded with marketing tracking built in. Mobile devices have all the added features with the ability to turn them on or off at your beck and call.

Even the cable companies track what we watch. You can run, but you can't hide from new products like Eyelock which work using biometric and digital recognition of your eye. Other deterrents include a digital fingerprint to log into your computer instead of using a password.

New phone applications for depositing checks electronically are a growing commodity in the fast-paced world of the wired consumer. These types of applications are still in the preliminary stages, but highly in demand by consumers. Saving time by banking electronically is a plus for everyone involved.

Web Footprints Can Reveal Much about a Skip, including the Location of Hidden Assets

An Internet profile reveals where we've been on the Internet, including our interaction with social networking groups like LinkedIn or Facebook, and what groups, organizations, or associations we may be a member of. This is also known as an Internet footprint. I do not think we will be able to opt out of that. That would be like opting out of getting a driver's license.

Advanced methods of hiding activities on the Internet include hiding the IP address. In e-mail tracing, we trace e-mail messages back to the sender In an attempt to reveal the skip trace portal or IP identifiers even when sometimes masking, spoofing, and redirecting can occur. The skip trace portal is the doorway to the website. It is really just an address. One example would be similar to the layout of a department store. There are many entrances to a store. It depends on which entrance you are talking about. When I go to Macy's, I usually go in at the main entrance. That entrance is the one on Thirty-Fourth Street and Broadway and leads me to the handbags section. That entrance is now closed due to a renovation, and I have to go into the store through another entrance, which means I will enter into a different department. Now I walk into the jewelry department which is on the other end of the store. The same idea applies to the Internet. Each entrance is a different portal to enter a website on the Internet and has a different address called the IP identifer. This is also known as the Internet protocol address, and it has a number just like an address in the real world. If you know the right address, then you can find what you are looking for.

The web is still growing by leaps and bounds, and though many people respect their privacy, they unconsciously or in many cases consciously place information on the Internet that immediately becomes an open book to the entire world. Whatever we put up on the Internet is public information for anyone to see. Please consider this fact when planning your career path. Consider that future employers may want to know a little bit more about who you are or they may just want to verify the information you submitted to them on your résumé.

The Internet Is Full of Weirdo Creeps and Freaks Ready to Launch a Cyber Attack, so It Pays to Be Wary When Logging On

Beware of cyber attacks—these are actually terror attacks. Some newer and more sophisticated cyber scams will target victims selectively. They locate a person's voice on the web and then call a relative and try to get the unsuspecting relative to wire them money and expose everything about themselves. This one has popped up again. As always, be wary of phone callers requesting information. Someone who claims to be from Microsoft claims that they have been receiving reports that your computer's IP has been associated with viruses, and that in order to fix it they will need access to your PC (personal computer). They will also ask you for a credit card. This is a scam which could potentially expose your passwords on your PC and credit card information.

With cyber wars reaching new heights, deny cyber breaches with good Internet security. Norton and MacAfee are the leaders in this space. America's real threats are these new tenacious cyber codes. These cyber intrusions cost corporations, and in turn our government, billions of dollars a year. Even Mac's are not immune. Recently over half a million Apple computers were attacked by a bot net. Everything has been hacked, and even though we've made headway and busted many rings, we just nabbed another big national ring. To these criminals, it is just another daily obstacle to overcome and conquer— and that is what they live for. In other instances, they do it just for bragging rights or out of resentment.

An international cyber sting led by the FBI attracted criminals from around the world and led to thirty-seven arrests in what is believed to be a multi-million-dollar online financial fraud case called *Operation Card Shop.* This is the biggest successful cyber sting in history. Officials called the sting the largest coordinated international police action in history that targeted cyber crime. The cyber sting used a website created by federal law enforcement officials as the spiderweb that lured in the alleged criminals. It was dubbed "Operation Card Shop," officials said. The alleged fraudsters could buy and sell stolen credit card numbers, drivers licenses, and bank information on the website, as well as discuss general hacking techniques, officials said. Agents then identified the suspects and fanned out across four continents to make the arrests. Hundreds of millions of dollars in losses have been prevented and hundreds of thousands of credit card numbers have been protected from "carding" crimes.

Some cyber crime is aimed directly at our national security, hurting our infrastructure and public safety. A recent wave of attacks by the hackers also targets industries and damages the security of our markets, our bank accounts, our secrets, and our privacy.

Using Hard-to-Break Passwords Just Makes Good Sense

Cyber passwords is the key! Use a formula with a sequential feature for the sites that require regular changing of your password. This can be even more important than biometrics. Keep all your passwords in an address book. Use a binder so you can add pages. Write your user id and password in pencil so you can erase it and update it. Keep them alphabetically listed and add pages as needed. This will keep you secure in the event of a cyber breach, virus infection, or a stolen laptop. Just be aware that your skip is doing the same thing.

Social networking sites are the perfect target for these cyber attacks because cyber tracking is like cyber speaking. With digital medical records now available, let's hope for good policy versus bad policy so they don't just become inventory on the lists with people taking passwords and pin numbers to their grave.

Social Networking Websites Are a Skip Tracer's Best Friend

These social sites may not be effective for collections, but they are very effective for skipping. People expose everything about themselves on these social sites, including pictures and contact and location info. Their lives are public for the world to see. Social networking sites no doubt are a gold mine for people in the skip tracing business. I recently had a case against a debtor who was high up on the food chain. He sat on several international corporate boards. I was hired to do an international bank search, and the first place I checked was Facebook. There was a full profile with a picture and almost a full résumé. As it turned out, he had just been asked to serve at the board's request in the Far East for this international corporation. As soon as I saw which country that corporation was headquartered out of, I was able to determine where to do my search. I found the assets I was looking for right away because I knew where to search. If I was looking in the wrong place, I could not have found what I was seeking. The client wanted me to search in an entirely different place, and I saved that client lots in search fees and located huge amounts of liquid assets.

Most divorce filings have the word *Facebook* in them. Facebook has been used to serve papers and create public records and then lawsuits. If someone checks in on Facebook every day at 9:00 a.m., you might try to serve them there. If you are not looking to serve process and you just need to locate what city the person is in, you can get this information this way. If you were not sure if your subject is in California or Florida, this step will get you that information by inference. This would be the process of reaching a conclusion by reasoning and evidence. The addresses are different, just like the zip codes would be very different. Look up the Internet protocol (IP) location and see where they are. You can determine the range and at the very least determine the city and state of their location. My two favorite sites for this task are www.ipchicken.com or www.infosniper.net.

Just a few of my favorite social networking sites are listed below. Programs like http://hootsuite.com/ which is the leading social media dashboard to manage and measure your social networks will help you navigate the social networking universe on the Internet.

Bogger.com

Branchout.com

Buzzup.com

Cake_Financial

Classmates.com

Delicious.com

Digg.com

Facebook.com

Flickr.com

Friendfeed.com

Geni.com

Googleplus.com

Hi5.com

Lawtalk.com

LinkedIn.com

Mashable.com

Meetup.com/whatever

Mixx.com

Myspace.com

Naymz.com

Pinterest.com

Pipl.com

Plaxo.com

Quora.com

Referralkey.com

Reunion.com

Rssfeeds.com

Skispace.com

Spokeo.com

Stumbleupon.com

TalentTrove

Twello.com

Twitter.com

Wackle.com

Wayn.com

Widgets.com

Youtube.com

Tapping into Twitter, LinkedIn, and Facebook Makes Good Sense When Tracking a Skip

The Internet has become a vast great power, a presence in the lives of billions of people on this planet. We use it to do everything from buying a book to getting a date, and most everything else in between. The social networking websites like Facebook and LinkedIn that were once thought of as unusual are now considered part of the cyber scape. We can't even imagine when they weren't there. The good news for us as skip tracers is that people tend to put lots of private information up on those websites, and they don't seem to consider the consequences. I think it's actually pretty funny when I find skips on Facebook, and I then uncover how much effort they put into hiding basically every other facet of their lives. So, the point is that social media websites are very powerful tools for skip tracers, and the best of us take full advantage of them.

For example, I recently had a case against a debtor in Colorado. Unlike some, this particular individual did a good job of staying off the Internet in terms of leaving a trail. There was no Internet profile at all except for a business listing on Twitter. The debtor was a hairstylist according to her prior job. When I called the salon to see if she was in, they said she was out that day but would be back tomorrow. I had her! If I hadn't checked Twitter, I might have missed her. This is the reason that this step should never be omitted by any skip tracer. Always at the very least type the name into the search bar in Twitter. Every step we take, every move we make brings us closer to our desired result.

Twitterverse is the cyberspace area of Twitter. This naturally extends beyond twitter.com to anywhere you can Twitter. This microblogging service will only allow 140 characters per post. It does allow all kinds of sharing including picture, video, information, and more. Twitter can be a powerful tool in your toolbox.

A whole new language has come with the advent of Twitter. In fact, it's so unique that the organization has put out a dictionary called Twittonary that provides explanations of various Twitter-related words. You can search the entire Twitter Dictionary or by single word, using their letter of the alphabet in the list on the site (see the Twitter Links pages for the link). Here are some of my personal favorites:

Tweeple: Twitter people, Twitter members, Twitter users

Tweeps: Twitter people that follow each other from one social media/network to another

Tweetaholic: Someone addicted to Twitter, so much so that it may be an actual problem

Tweet-back: Bringing a previous tweet conversation or reference back into the current conversation

Tweet-dropping: Eavesdropping on someone else's home page in "friends" mode

Tweeterboxes: Twitterers who tweet too much

Tweetheart: That special tweeter who makes your heart skip a beat

Tweet(ing): The act of posting to Twitter

Twittering: To send a Twitter message

Twitterrhea: The act of sending too many Twitter messages

Twittermania is contagious, and it is easy to become a twittermaniac. If you are searching for your skip in twitter, and he is there, use as many of the utilities as possible in order to maximize its functionality.

Checking LinkedIn Will Likely Yield Excellent Results if the Skip Is Involved with Business

LinkedIn is the world's largest professional network with over 120 million members and growing rapidly. LinkedIn connects you to your contacts and helps you exchange knowledge, ideas, and opportunities with a broader network of professionals. Relationships matter, and this is the most business-oriented place to connect out there.

People on the Internet who are looking for a job or for clients or work go to LinkedIn first. This is just a known fact. LinkedIn is the only place online that is strictly business! This is one of the most important steps the skip tracer will take. This step will show you a person's background. It will tell you the field of business that they are in. It will also tell you if they are working or if they are looking for work. It will tell you more about their work history than you could have ever imagined. It will even tell you dates of employment. LinkedIn is a powerful locator tool because the information is directly from the source. Your subject entered that information about themselves in that space. We can use it as part of our search by searching for the person by name and then narrowing the search to geographical area. I use LinkedIn every day in my business, and it is a preferred and valuable resource tool in my life.

LinkedIn gives you the keys to controlling your online identity. Have you Googled yourself lately? You never know what may come up. LinkedIn profiles rise to the top of search results, letting you control the first impression people get when searching for you online. This international company is much more than just a social networking online meeting place. You can find customers, jobs, list jobs, read résumés, join industry groups, follow companies and members. Skip tracers can even find other things as a byproduct.

In June 2012, about 6.5 million LinkedIn passwords were likely hacked, in what will probably serve as a big wake-up call for all social networks to upgrade their security. LinkedIn bears responsibility in this case, since the site didn't properly encrypt its password database. Any site that requires passwords is susceptible to this. So make your passwords as strong as possible.

In today's professional world, people change jobs and locations constantly. By connecting on LinkedIn, your address book will never go out of date. Your contacts update their profiles, keeping you current with their latest jobs, projects, and contact info. You'll stay in closer contact with great tools to communicate and collaborate.

Going to Facebook in the Beginning of a Skip Trace Makes Good Sense

Facebook is a wonderful treasure trove of all kinds of intriguing data for a skip tracer like you! Facebook is still free, and some businesses take advantage of that to put up free websites for their business. I recently found a towing company and the owner in Florida on Facebook. It was the only Internet profile I could find. The photo of the debtor with his tow truck and logo advertising his business was on his new timeline. I was able to track down this deadbeat by focusing on the step that I had to take. As you go through all the steps, you will begin to gather information to put everything together to reach your goal.

Facebook was ranked as the most-used social networking service by worldwide active users. Just in its infant state, in the world of public companies, Facebook is planning a deeper push into search. It is already planning to crawl and then stand up and then walk and run—and finally to race with the big boys. They let a girl into the all-boys club. It will be improving search for the site. It had for a very short time, "search for friends nearby," but that was taken down in order to make room for the new and improved search. Searching the social network could get a lot better in the near future. Stay tuned for more.

With over nine hundred million (and counting) users worldwide, Facebook is one of the leading destinations influencing online identity, entertainment, and content distribution. Facebook is your playbook to get the most out of the rich opportunities to skip trace successfully in the Facebook ecosystem. The United States has 157.3 million members since June 2012 as this book goes to print.

The Facebook Camera, a new mobile app that makes using Facebook photos faster and easier, is already available and widely used. So after you find your skip, you can view the photos. They have had video calling available since July 2011. They also have had voice calling and messaging since April 2011.

Users may join common-interest user groups that are organized by workplace, school or college, or other characteristics, and categorize their friends into lists such as "People from Work" or "Close Friends."

Facebook has allowed us to stay in touch with friends, relatives, and other acquaintances wherever they are in the world, as long as there is access to the Internet. Some studies have named Facebook as a source of problems in relationships. Several news stories have suggested that using Facebook can lead to higher instances of divorce and infidelity, but those claims have been questioned. That would be like saying that you are obese because you eat super-size meals at the fast-food restaurants. On the flipside of that thought is that maybe super-size was created to give a better deal to the obese. Either way, the fact is that most divorce proceedings have the word *Facebook* in them. If you search for "Facebook" and "divorce" and read the results in your search results, you can see this for yourself. That does not mean that is the cause for the divorce, maybe just a symptom. The details are there for the world to see. Think about what you share on Facebook and remember that when you are looking for your subject—they know it.

Researchers wanted to find out if Facebook might be making us feel better about ourselves. In an experiment, a group of 151 college students were randomly assigned the job of editing their Facebook or MySpace page or completing a task through Google Maps. The study showed that those who edited their MySpace page showed increased narcissism. Those who edited their Facebook page showed greater self-esteem. Facebook is probably the most loved space in cyberspace.

Social media websites are among the most powerful resources a skip tracer can access, and they should always be included very early in a search. Harnessing the power of search engines like Google is simply part of a skip tracer's job. Bring the power of the Internet to bear on your goal, and you'll get the results you are looking for.

> It's a sure thing that you'll not finish if you don't start.
>
> —Napoleon Hill

Chapter 9
Links You Can Use

The modern skip tracer relies heavily on the Internet. In fact, I would argue that at no other time has skip tracing been so effective, and it's all because of the power of the Internet. Much of your day will be spent doing research on a computer, surfing from one website to another as you track down deadbeats and search for their hidden assets. To assist you, I've put together a comprehensive list of all kinds of useful links. Included are my insights about the various types of links, descriptions of the websites, and occasionally a review.

Databases

The following links to large databases play a part in many of my skip traces. The data is open- and closed-source.

http://www.tuc.com/ Trans Union serves both consumers and the business world, providing accurate credit and fraud-prevention data, and information-based solutions. To order your free credit report call (800) 888-4213.

http://www.equifax.com/ Equifax's global operations include consumer and commercial credit information services. To order your free credit report call (800) 685-1111.

http://www.experian.com/ Experian is a supplier of consumer and business credit, direct marketing, and automotive and real estate information services. To order your free credit report call (888) 397-3742.

http://www.dnb.com/ Dun & Bradstreet has the largest selection of information on private companies. Products and services are drawn from a global database of more than ninety-four million companies. One of the skip tracer's best friends.

http://www.nexis.com/research Lexis-Nexis is the world's largest provider of credible, in-depth information. From legal and government to business and high-tech, their products and services provide direct access to an enormous information universe.

http://www.hoovers.com/free Contains the *Corporate Directory*, which can be searched by ticker symbol, company name, location, industry and/or sales. This database profiles publicly listed US companies traded on the three major stock exchanges and more than 1,200 of America's largest private companies. This site also has many links to other useful resources and is now a D&B company.

http://www.bankruptcydata.com/Courts/NewYork.htm Offers powerful products designed to meet the needs of bankruptcy and credit professionals. Performs a *free* search of public company bankruptcies.

http://www.knowx.com/ KnowX.com provides real-time access to billions of public records, private records, and assets. Now part of Choicepoint, it still provides a free FEIN search. Reed Elsevier, the owner of the LexisNexis information service, has purchased this asset, which was announced on February 21, 2008, and which will result in higher-quality information.

http://www.zoominfo.com/ Zoominfo, formerly Eliyon Technologies, provides a comprehensive source of information on business professionals. This growing database currently contains over nineteen million executives, managers, and professionals in 1,192,634 companies—all instantly searchable to meet your needs. Provides free searches.

http://www.guidestar.org/ Guidestar generates and distributes extensive programmatic and financial information about more than 850,000 American charitable nonprofit organizations. The website is a free, public Internet service and is the nation's leading source of information about nonprofit organizations. View Form 990—dig deep for officers and board of directors, compensation, packages, and much more.

http://www.firstdatacorp.com/ Provides electronic funds transfers to 75 percent of the world and provides card issuer services for 1,400 financial institutions and more than 390 million consumers worldwide. About 1,100 transactions are handled every second of every day—a company with conviction. Do the math—that is giganormous. They are the source information provider to the info world, and they surpass their peers. It is always higher quality information.

http://www.tlo.com/ As the new kid on the block and as the competition stiffens amongst the information data providers, here is a database that has positioned itself for growth because it has combined price and quality. We asked for it and we got it—they have photos available! Now that is progress!

http://www.feinsearch.com/ Provides federal employer identification number for a fee from Form 5500, which is the source. Batching is available.

Public Records

Public records are documents that are not considered confidential. For example, when someone is born, a public record is created and those records can be accessed. A public record will become public record when it is recorded in the corresponding jurisdiction.

Any document that is required by law to be created or maintained is a public record. They are created when people file suits in court or as a result of public filings like bankruptcies, liens, judgments, encumbrances, property records, trademarks and patents, and more. Information obtained from local, state, or federal courts indicating a person's history of meeting financial obligations, including alimony and child support, are also public record. The same holds true for companies. Information on your credit report that has been obtained from public court records such as bankruptcies, judgments, and liens. This applies to businesses as well.

Public records are different from government records because some of those are not public. Social Security information is not public and is a government record as one example, although they will verify if a Social Security number is valid.

Where there are assets, there are records of those assets. These records can be accessed by the general public, as they relate to a consumer's obligations. Assets like homes, equipment, tractors, boats, aircraft, chattels (co-ops and condos), and other securitized or collateralized assets all have UCC or other public record filings which can be used to locate them.

Access to public records to anyone who wishes to view them has dramatically increased in the days of digital information. Third parties such as the information broker industry make regular use of public records to compile profiles on millions of people that are easily accessible to anyone at the click of a mouse, and sometimes make a profit from the service of recompiling and mining the data.

Google tools and applications like Google earth, Google maps, Google visual, and Sidewiki are just a few of the resources at your fingertips to search the public records. Obstacles are those frightful things you see when you take your eyes off the goal. So keep on tracing.

http://www.edgar-online.com/start.asp   From   the Edgar Database you can retrieve SEC filings (including 10K's, 10Q's, annual reports, and prospectuses) for approximately 3,500 US public corporations.

http://www.sec.gov/edgar.shtml The SEC requires all public companies to file registration statements, periodic reports, and other forms electronically through Edgar. Anyone can access and download this information for free.

http://www.brbpub.com/pubrecsites.asp Search over 650 state, county, city, and federal court URLs, where you can access public record information free.

http://www.governmentfilesonline.com/home/ Governmentfilesonline.com lists Secretary of State websites to search and file online public records for entities in all states.

http://www.publicrecordfinder.com This search engine is dedicated to locating worldwide public records.

http://www.searchsystems.net/ This is the first and continues to be the largest collection of free public records on the Internet. This was formerly pac-info.

http://www.recordsbase.com/resources is a leading source of genealogy resources, vital record searches, and online family trees. They seek to make many genealogy resources and public records easily accessible to all. It also has a good military search.

http://www.networksolutions.com/whois-search/netsol. com "Who is" query by NetSol is available by IP address or domain name lookup. Actively monitor any domain and receive notification of all their ongoing activity. This was formerly Intenic, who was the original provider of IP addresses. This is the oldest and the original source.

http://www.zocdoc.com/ Find a doctor and make an appointment online. I love seeing the photos of the doctors. A picture is worth a thousand words.

http://www.findadoc.com/ FindaDoc provides free access to over 720,000 doctors in the United States.

http://www.nurse.net/ The mission of NP Central is to provide reliable and useful clinical, organizational, educational, and job-related information in a usable, convenient format to nurse practitioners, as well as legislators, consumers, and others who are seeking information about nurse practitioners.

http://patft.uspto.gov/ Official search for issued patents and patent applications.

http://tess2.uspto.gov/ TESS is the official Trademark Electronic Search System, and it contains more than four million pending, registered, and dead federal trademarks.

http://www.copyright.gov/records/ Search records of registered books, music, art, periodicals, and other works. It includes copyright and ownership documents. The site covers works registered and documents recorded by the US Copyright Office since January 1, 1978.

Government Records

Government records are all books, papers, maps, photographs, machine-readable materials, or other documentary materials, regardless of physical form or characteristics, made or received by an agency of the United States Government under federal law or in connection with the transaction of public business and preserved or appropriate for preservation by that agency or its legitimate successor as evidence of the organization, functions, policies, decisions, procedures, operations, or other activities of the government or because of the informational value of the data in them. Library and museum material made or acquired and preserved solely for reference or exhibition purposes, extra copies of documents preserved only for convenience of reference and stocks of publications and of processed documents are not included.

Vision is the art of seeing things invisible. Government records are not all public but can still be searched. They are the result of births, marriages, divorces, deaths, and motor vehicle transactions. They are created when you get a license in so many different specialties, activities, or hobbies. A few types of government records that are created on a daily basis include driving, real estate, private investigation, medicine, dentistry, nursing, accounting, law, fishing, brokers, and other professions.

Compilation is work formed by the collection and assembling of preexisting materials or of data that are selected, coordinated, or arranged in such a way that the resulting work as a whole constitutes an original work of authorship. The term *compilation* includes collective works. You can compile a wealth of information from government records.

Operational records are those that reflect the unique mandate of their creators. Records of programs, projects, and service delivery are examples of operational records. Unlike corporate records, these will be different in each organization. Search these well. These are a must for every skip tracer because we want to find interoffice communications that can shed some light on a possible time period. If you know your deadbeat worked for the government, then you would need to further narrow down that information and this would be one path to examine. For example, if he worked in the service delivery area, then he might be a shipping or warehouse clerk.

If you know someone's profession, you can find where they work. A wise man turns chance into fortune. So if you think you can win, you can win. Faith is necessary to victory. You need to stay on the path to your goals.

http://www.ssa.gov/ Use the Social Security Administration to help you locate your missing person. The Social Security office can be very resourceful in understanding Social Security law, history, and planning of the agency.

http://www.ancestry.com/search/rectype/vital/ssdi/main.htm Search millions of names in the Social Security Death Index at Ancestry.com, the most up-to-date SSDI on the Internet.

http://www.statelocalgov.net/ State and local government on the net is a frequently updated directory of links to government sponsored and controlled resources on the Internet.

http://www.marriagedatabase.com/ Marriage records have been a great help to many genealogy and family history researchers, providing valuable information and clues to an ancestor's or relative's marriage. Over the last few years, many people and organizations have been publishing marriage record archives on the Internet—some with thousands of records, others with millions. Presented on this website are individual "State Guides" designed to show you where all the best marriage record archives and databases are found. This is not an official government site.

http://www.divorcerecordsusa.com/ The easiest online divorce record ordering system on the Internet is found here. Do you need to verify that a divorce has been filed or finalized? This can be used for religious, legal, genealogical, or journalistic reasons.

http://www.vitalchek.com VitalChek is your official source for government-issued vital records. With secure online ordering, partnerships throughout the country, and quick turnaround, they're the one to trust. When you need birth certificates or marriage, divorce, or death records,

VitalChek (a Lexis Nexis company) is your number-one source.

https://www.usavital.com/ Use this to locate birth certificates, death certificates, marriage certificates, and divorce documents that are filed as public records with the state, county, commonwealth, or territory.

http://courtreference.com/ Access to trial court records varies from state to state, and many trial courts offer online access to court records or court case information through statewide judiciary or individual court websites.

http://www.fedstats.gov/ which has been available to the public since 1997, provides access to the full range of official statistical information produced by the federal government.

http://www.statenet.com/ State Net (a Lexis Nexis company) tracks tens of thousands of bills in all fifty states, US Congress, and the District of Columbia, at any given time.

http://www.ncsc.org/default.aspx The National Center for State Courts is a valuable resource for public filings and government records.

http://www.health.state.ny.us/nysdoh/consumer/vr.htm This is the vital records search information site for New York State. Search for birth, death, marriage, and divorce records.

http://www.op.nysed.gov/opsearches.htm Use this New York State site to verify and archive licensure and professional disciplinary actions. It has *free searches.*

http://appext9.dos.ny.gov/lcns_public/chk_load This is an index of licensees and registrants from the New York State Department of State.

http://www.dos.ny.gov/licensing/ The New York Department of State's Division of Licensing Services (DLS) oversees the licensure, registration, and regulation of twenty-nine occupations throughout the state. DLS licenses over eight hundred thousand individuals including real estate brokers, notaries, private investigators, and appearance enhancement professionals. Through its licensing and business filing capacities, the division promotes business growth while protecting the health, safety, and welfare of all New Yorkers.

http://iapps.courts.state.ny.us/attorney/AttorneySearch The New York State attorney directory search is provided as a *free* public service by the New York State Unified Court System.

http://www.courts.state.ny.us/ Search the New York State Unified Court System.

Criminal Records

Skip tracing the criminal records gives extra value to your work and your perspective. It helps to paint a clearer picture of your skip. Don't forget to search these. The primary benefit of using these criminal links is the ability to get a handle on the criminal background, if any, of the skip we are trying to find. Protect yourself, your family, and your children as a secondary benefit. Databases serve as a focal point in providing assistance to parents, children, law enforcement, schools, and the community in identification of potential sex offenders. These types have criminal minds and are some of the worst offenders because they destroy children's lives, which destroys everyone else's lives.

Criminal background checks are not a substitute for your own due diligence. You must use research or caution when investigating others. The reports strive to provide the most helpful information; they do not represent or warrant that the results are 100 percent accurate or up to date. There may be criminal history, arrest records, sex offender registry data, and/or other public records that are not present in database results for a variety of reasons, and you should be aware of such possibilities.

With new technologies like digital surveillance and photos on the Internet, criminal records are changing in nature. What once took a long time and was labor intensive, now takes just a few moments. To rate these snakes you'll need powerful tools.

http://www.bop.gov/ Federal Bureau of Prisons may be searched by name or identification number. This is a nationwide search.

http://www.criminalsearches.com/ Use this to narrow your search using middle name, county, year of birth, or age range.

www.myinmatelocator.com MyInmatelocator.com is your all-inclusive website for finding inmates and prisoners who are incarcerated in local, state, or federal correctional institutes. On this site you will find portals to Department of Corrections websites, inmate locators, and information on jails and prisons.

http://www.mugshots.com/ Mugshots.com is a search engine for official law enforcement records, specifically booking photographs and mug shots. This information was originally collected and distributed by law enforcement agencies. Mugshots.com republishes these official records in their original form. The freedom to publish true and factual information is allowed due to the Freedom of Information Act. This contains public arrest records with images.

http://www.bustedmugshots.com/ On this website you will find mug shots of people who have been arrested and charged with a crime.

http://www.inmate-search.org/ Locate and find details on practically any inmate in the United States. Search for past and present inmates who live and work around you right now.

http://arrestrecords.us.com/ Search to see if they have been arrested for any serious crimes that may alert you to possible danger. This site is wonderful if you are trying to discover the facts about someone who may be a danger to you and your family.

https://www.instantcheckmate.com/ Their goal is to provide you with the most useful, detailed, and important information on just about anyone. Whether researching criminal history, phone numbers, addresses, demographic data, census data, or a wide variety of other information, they help thousands of Americans find what they're looking for.

http://www.sexoffender.com/search.htm Criminal background records will help you find out who that new neighbor is down the street. They may know you, your children ... what do you know about them?

http://www.sexoffenderregistry.net/ Enter your zip code to locate offenders in your neighborhood. Other searches are available at a premium.

http://www.familywatchdog.us/ Family Watchdog is a free service to help locate registered sex offenders in your area. They encourage you to use their site to help educate your family on possible dangers. If you are looking for a skip who is sexual predator, you can get free alerts on him.

Military Records

A military record is the history applied to the military personnel in the armed forces. Finding military records can be helpful for skip tracing research. Sometimes our skip is deployed and then we must stop all collection activity. Our most important considerations are if the subject is active or inactive, what are the active duty dates, and are they waiting to be deployed again. Also, what branch of the military did they serve in is a special issue to consider. Privacy considerations exempt financial information from being disclosed. You also have to comply with the Servicemembers Civil Relief Act.

http://www.dod.mil/pubs/foi/ This Requester Service Center (RSC) processes Freedom of Information Act (FOIA) requests for records related to the Office of the Secretary of Defense. The mission of the Office of Freedom of Information is to provide access to records created by the Office of the Secretary of Defense and Joint Staff.

http://militarypay.defense.gov/ The Military Pay and Benefits website is sponsored by the Office of the Undersecretary of Defense for Personnel and Readiness. Currently, the major elements of compensation are discussed.

http://www.defense.gov/ Formerly at www.dod.mil.gov, this is the new Department of Defense website.

http://www.familymilitaryrecords.com/ You can use both first and last name to get a more refined result list, or just use the last name to get back a more broad result list. Use the genealogy directory. This is powered by www.myfamily.com.

http://www.searchmil.com/ A military search directory.

http://www.militarysearch.com/ They limit retrieval to documents or information available from a public entity or public utility that are intended for public use.

http://www.vetfriends.com/ Search by first and last name or join and get unlimited access.

http://www.military.com/ Since 1999, their free membership has connected service members, military families, and veterans to all the benefits of service— government benefits, scholarships, discounts, lifelong friends, mentors, great stories of military life or missions, and much more. They are also the largest military and veteran membership organization—ten million members strong.

http://vfw.org You can search the veterans of foreign wars on this site.

http://www.recordsbase.com/resources/military-records Even with the Internet, locating military records can take a great deal of time because you have to search through a variety of resources. You can take your search to the National Archives Building in Washington, DC, for the original records.

http://www.archives.gov/veterans/military-service-records/ This will access online military personnel records request system via eVetRecs batch processing.

http://www.archives.com/ Archives.com represents an affordable and powerful solution to any family history researcher, from beginner to expert.

http://www.archives.gov/st-louis/military-personnel/foia-info.html#mprfoia Use this site to further understand what information is available to the general public. The National Personnel Records Center and Military Personnel Records Center is the repository of millions of military personnel records of discharged and deceased veterans of all services during the twentieth century, post–World War I.

http://www.usa.gov/ This site will provide instructions and procedures for obtaining military records.

http://www.togetherweserved.com/ The largest exclusively military network of its type, Together We Served enables veterans and active duty personnel to reconnect with lost brothers and sisters, share in the camaraderie of other servicemen and women, and create a permanent record of their service so this may never be forgotten.

http://www.militaryonesource.mil/MOS/f?p=MOS:HOME:0 This is powered by www.usa.gov. Use it to search for different branches.

http://www.militarybenefit.org/ Military Benefit Organization is dedicated to providing members with great options for benefits.

http://military-veteran.com/ An online directory for all the branches.

https://www.nationalresourcedirectory.gov/ This will connect wounded warriors, service members, veterans, their families, and caregivers with those who support them.

http://www.gisearch.com/ GI Search is a military locator and community with over 140,000 members and photos.

http://www.vetbiz.gov/ This is the US Department of Veterans Affairs presence on the Internet.

http://www.navy.mil/ This is the source for all information about the Navy.

http://www.army.mil/ Visit this site for information about the Army.

http://www.af.mil/ Here is the official site of the US Air Force. The Air Force Personnel Center provides information about locating military personnel currently serving in the United States Air Force (USAF) through the Air Force Worldwide Locator.

http://www.marines.mil/Pages/ The official US Marines website is the place to be for information about the US Marines.

http://www.uscg.mil/ This US Coast Guard site has all the resources you will need to research that branch of the service.

Corporate Links

Corporate records are often referred to as administrative records. These are created by all organizations to support administrative functions, including human resources, general administration, facilities management, financial management, information and information technology management, and equipment and supplies material management. The value of these records is consistent across the government sector and the private sector. To the skip tracer, these are priceless.

Corporate searches for publically traded companies are relatively simple because the Securities and Exchange Commission requires quarterly reporting of financial statements. This information is free and open to anyone who wants to see it. Not-for-profit corporations and charities also have open books, and the tax returns are available online. You can search for all the facts and figures and see details on compensation of officers and bonuses to officers. You can check for related party transactions and see which members of the board sit on other boards of the competition. You can check for subsidiaries and spin-off companies as well as holding companies, trust companies, off shore companies, and shell companies. You can check the notes to financial statements for pending litigation and other forecasts based on history and performance. Pending litigation could put a company out of business if they don't have the funds to defend themselves. Sometimes particular parties are named in specific lawsuits, and if that is the skip you are looking for, then that is important information. Your skip might have to resign.

Forecasts will let you know if and when any sites will be closed due to poor performance or due to regulations or other variables. Scanning financial statements can sometimes be the difference between finding your skip and missing out by not looking in the right place.

Corporate searches for closely held private corporations are not public. This information is guarded by the board members. Because these closely guarded secrets do not need to be reported to the public and the competition, it is more difficult to gather valuable information. This is where we need to dig deeper. Espionage of one form or another can be used to obtain information that is not readily available. From persuasion to brainwashing—we can walk into the place of business and buy what they sell and get tons of tracing done all in one shot. We have a reservoir of ability that typically goes untouched. We must try to awaken our individual potential and realize that with knowledge comes power.

When it comes to corporate records, some information is available and some information is not available at all. When we try to master the techniques that the pros use, we are looking for facts that lead us to the truth. What's funny about truth is that it depends on the perspective. Is the glass half full or half empty? It is impossible to determine exactly unless we actually measure the number of ounces. We are looking for information that will provide details into the corporate intricacies. We need to determine the shareholders' names and uncover their background. Also, we need to identify the assets of the corporation in terms of capital assets as well as human capital. Every piece of information you gather will take you to the next step. Every piece to the puzzle will give you a better edge in solving the puzzle. Even if you are missing a few pieces of the puzzle, you can still see the big picture.

http://www.businesscreditusa.com/index.asp This is now owned by Credit.net and will verify existing business with *free searches on twelve million businesses*! It is powered by infoUSA.

http://www.corporationwiki.com/ Search by company or by individual.

http://www.corporateinformation.com/ It allows users to search for companies by name, location, or industry. This site will provide phone number, ownership structure, ticker symbol, and link to company home page.

http://www.bbb.org/BBBComplaints/lookup.asp Better Business Bureau has business reports that include time in business, complaint history, and information obtained through special bureau investigations. Charity reports include information on the group's background, current programs, governing body, fund-raising practices, tax-exempt status, and finances. *Fee based!*

http://www.thomasnet.com/ The Directory of American Manufacturers was formerly Thomas Register and has renovated its website for easier use.

http://www.cjr.org/tools/owners/ Who Owns What is *Columbia Journalism Review*'s online guide to what major media companies own.

http://www.standardpoor.com/ Standard & Poor's is a leader in business information and rating service. They rate companies the way that the credit bureaus rate individuals.

http://www.moodys.com/ Moody's is an essential component of the global capital markets, providing credit ratings, research, tools, and analysis that contribute to transparent and integrated financial markets. Moody's Corporation (NYSE: MCO) is the parent company of Moody's Investors Service, which provides credit ratings and research covering debt instruments and securities, and Moody's Analytics, which offers leading-edge software, advisory services, and research for credit and economic analysis and financial risk management. The corporation, which reported revenue of $2.3 billion in 2011, employs approximately 6,400 people worldwide and maintains a presence in 28 countries.

http://www.fitchratings.com/ Fitch Ratings is a global rating agency dedicated to providing value beyond the rating through independent and prospective credit opinions, research, and data. They are responsible for rating countries and downgrading credit ratings from AAA to AA as they did to the US.

http://www.nyse.com/ The New York Stock Exchange strives to be an educator and a resource for the investment community. To achieve that goal, they have created a special section for novice investors, a designated area for the press, easy access to market data, and links to NYSE-listed company websites. It is now a public company.

http://www.irs.gov/charities/index.html Search the Internal Revenue Service website for charities and nonprofits.

http://www.charitynavigator.org/ Charity Navigator is America's premier independent charity evaluator. It works to advance a more efficient and responsive philanthropic marketplace by evaluating the financial health of over 5,500 of America's largest charities.

http://www.marketresearch.com/ Marketresearch is an aggregate of global business intelligence representing the most comprehensive collection of published market research available.

http://www.aaag.com/ America at a Glance lets you search over eighteen million businesses free.

http://www.braintrack.com/ The web's most complete directory for university and college searches. Operating since 1996, they list over ten thousand higher education institutions in 194 countries, and the list is continually updated with new resources for education. This is not a corporate search, but it will show what resources are available to you.

http://www.chamberofcommerce.com/ Provides information on 14MM businesses from more than one hundred online and offline sources of information. In partnership with companies like Google, Yahoo, Bing, Acxiom, Yelp, CitySearch, Localeze & Superpages, ChamberofCommerce.com provides tools and solutions to help business develop and manage their business on the web.

http://www.uschamber.com/ The US Chamber of Commerce is the world's largest business federation representing the interests of more than three million businesses of all sizes, sectors, and regions, as well as state and local chambers and industry associations.

http://www.companylink.com/ Research and contacts for public companies. It is powered by SmartName to bring you targeted search terms designed specifically to enhance the user's overall online search experience. Companylink.com displays the top advertisers and more. They've taken the confusion out of searching online, allowing you to find what you want in a timely manner.

http://www.coordinatedlegal.com/SecretaryOfState.html Links for legal professionals and others who are looking for quick access to the corporate information available in online searchable databases.

http://www.score.org/ Counselors of America's Small Business Owners is a national association dedicated to helping small business owners form and grow their businesses.

http://www.usabusinessdirectories.com/ Over six hundred US and international business directories to choose from! Great business-to-business resource.

http://www.muckety.com/ Muckety is an award-winning website and information/technology company, honored for outstanding use of digital technologies. Unlike most social networking sites, the data is not user contributed.

http://www.ziggs.com/ Founded on the principles of professionalism and respect, Ziggs' community serves people around the world. Search for professionals with this people search from an index of 2,721,696 professionals representing 83,897 companies.

http://www.zibb.com/ Strictly business is the global business search engine. It's the business-to-business search engine of Reed Business, the premier provider of business information to the world. It includes content from across the entire Reed Business portfolio with the addition of selected business-to-business websites outside of Reed Business. They are the largest business-to-business publisher in the world. We have a portfolio of more than two hundred market leading publications, newsletters, directories and reference books, electronic products, online services, industry conferences, and awards.

Social Media

Twitter and LinkedIn each have associated links that will be helpful to you.

Twitter

Twitter was founded in March 2006 by San Francisco start-up company Obvious Corp. There are several books, webinars, tutorials, and more dedicated to learning

Twitter. The Twitter Guide Book by www.Mashable.com is the best seller in this area. Stay up to date in your field by searching Twitter feeds!

http://www.tweetdeck.com/ TweetDeck is an app that brings more flexibility and insight to power users.

http://www.twellow.com/ Twellow is a directory of public Twitter accounts, with hundreds of categories and search features to help you find people who matter to you. The Twitter yellow pages.

http://www.twinitor.com/ Twinitor is a Twitter search and monitoring. You can search any kind of information real time (any keywords and phrases, twitter #tags and @ users). The tool allows you to monitor a set of different keywords at same time!

http://mytwitterdirectory.com/ My Twitter Directory is the Twitter Yellow Pages.

http://tweet.grader.com/ Twitter Grader is a free tool that allows you to check the power of your Twitter profile compared to millions of other users that have been graded. Twitter Grader algorithm and associated rankings is based on a quantitative assessment of your reach and influence in the Twitter community, based on your interactions with others and the frequency of posts. You can also search for users by location. It goes down to city and state … That is nice.

http://tweetgrade.com/ Find somebody on Twitter that you want to follow but aren't sure if they're worth your valuable "follow"? Or just want to get the word out there about your TweetGrade? This is the place for that tool.

http://twittonary.com/ Having twissues with your twerminology? Check out the Twitter dictionary (Twittonary).

LinkedIn

http://learn.linkedin.com/what-is-linkedin/ The training center is chock full of nuts and bolts. This is a walk through the park. They also have user guides for the following sectors: small business; new users; students; job seekers; entrepreneurs; attorneys; business development; consultants journalists; nonprofits; venture capital.

http://learn.linkedin.com/training/ Learn how to complete your profile, participate in groups, adjust your settings, search LinkedIn. A free training webinar designed exclusively for group owners and managers, you will learn the strategies and best practices to running a successful group. Learn how to utilize all the tools of LinkedIn Company Pages to give your company a powerful online presence. Learn how to download apps for your mobile devices. Learn about the unique tools LinkedIn offers to Pro members.

http://www.linkedin.com/answers Need an answer? Ask a question here. In the whirlwind of new market changes, stay ahead of the curve and ask technical questions that you can use to seek the information you need.

http://www.linkedin.com/today/ The day's top news, tailored for you. Review your key options on a daily basis.

http://blog.linkedin.com/ This concise blog will help you maintain your expertise and advise clients what options are available to them.

http://www.linkedin.com/static?key=microsoft_outlook This app will let you get LinkedIn for Outlook. Get more info about your important contacts, see what they're doing, and stay in touch. The LinkedIn app gives you access to your professional network from your Android device.

Financial Records

Financial searches can be performed on the *creditor*. If your subject owns a property and if the property has a mortgage, the mortgage application can be obtained by serving an information subpoena on the bank. The response will yield all the evidence you are looking for and then some. You will get all of the bank account information including account numbers and insurance policies in different types and classes. We have asset types and asset classes with subcategories in each that can discover hidden assets.

Financial searches can be done on the *lender* and on *loan modification packages* and *refinances*. These will supply bank account information and bank account numbers as well as other equity.

Financial searches can be done by serving the *landlord* and figuring out how much of a deposit is held at what bank as well as how the rent is paid. This evidence can be had with a subpoena.

Financial searches can be done on *divorce records*. These can be a gold mine of information when personal net worth statements and schedules of assets are discovered. In most cases, divorce records are public information. This varies on a state-by-state basis. In some states you must be a party to the action to get access.

Financial searches can be conducted on *tax liens*. If a property is owned and taxes are delinquent, many counties and cities turn them over for cash. Since they are not receiving the revenue from the tax roll and they generally need the funds to pay for costs like municipal employees' salaries and benefits, they will sell off the asset to the highest bidder in the form of a tax lien. Those tax liens contain your freedom and success.

Financial searches can be conducted on *civil records* to uncover information such as current or past financial restitution cases, personal injury, and civil disputes. These figures are an extremely positive indicator of the quality and range of the asset quality of the hard and soft assets.

Financial searches can be done on a *bankruptcy.* Bankruptcy is a public proceeding, and they don't know the wealth of information they have left behind. Even if your debtor filed bankruptcy eight years ago, the records may still be online. If the bank information is old, a lot of debtors have trouble switching to a new bank because the new banks don't want them.

Financial searches can be accomplished by serving the *insurance company.* Often times while insurance policies may not be garnishable, the proceeds from a settlement can be intercepted.

These are some of the financial assets that can yield hidden treasures—because everyone needs insurance. Everyone needs an insurance broker to locate secret and protected assets. These are so exciting that you have to run out to skip trace some:

> *auto liability insurance, assumption reinsurance, auto repair insurance, aviation insurance, bond insurance, builder's risk insurance, business interruption insurance, business overhead expense, business umbrella insurance, disability insurance, casualty insurance, catastrophe bond, charge-back insurance, computer insurance, contents insurance, credit insurance, crime insurance, death bond, deposit insurance, directors and officers liability insurance, earthquake insurance, employer defense insurance, employment insurance, errors and omissions insurance, fidelity bond, fi-*

nancial reinsurance, flood insurance, general insurance, group insurance, guaranteed asset protection insurance, health insurance, home insurance, income protection insurance, inland marine insurance, interest rate insurance, intellectual property insurance, key person insurance, kidnap and ransom insurance, landlords insurance, legal expenses insurance, lenders mortgage insurance, liability insurance, income life insurance, locked funds insurance, longevity bond, longevity insurance, marine insurance, mortgage insurance, mutual insurance, no-fault insurance, parametric insurance, payment protection insurance, pension insurance, pension term assurance, perpetual insurance, personal liability insurance, pet insurance, political risk insurance, pollution insurance, pre-paid legal service, prize indemnity insurance, professional liability insurance, property insurance, protection and indemnity insurance, reinsurance, rent guarantee insurance, satellite insurance, terminal illness insurance, terrorism insurance, title insurance, trade credit insurance, travel insurance, UCC insurance, uninsured employer insurance, workers' compensation insurance, unit-linked insurance plan, wage insurance, war risk insurance, weather insurance, worker's compensation insurance, the Zombie fund

http://www.investopdia.com/ An encyclopedia of investment terms and more.

http://www.investorglossary.com/ Investor Glossary is loaded with helpful investment information and is updated frequently.

http://www.investorwords.com/ InvestorWords is the premier financial glossary on the web, helping millions of individuals understand and keep up-to-date with the terms that they need to know in order to succeed in today's financial world. InvestorWords.com is operated by WebFinance Inc.

http://www.orderannualreports.com/ The Annual Reports Service is a free service provided by PrecIsionIR. II provides quick access to annual reports and other information on select companies.

http://www.orderfundinfo.com/ The Fund Info Service provides quick access to prospectuses and other information on select funds for free from PrecisionIR. Search by alpha, fund family, or investment objective.

http://www.fakechecks.org/ National Consumers League is a central source of information and advice about fake check scams.

http://www.finra.org/ The Financial Industry Regulatory Authority is the largest nongovernmental securities regulator for all US securities firms.

http://www.sipc.org/ The Securities Investor Protection Corporation helps to restore funds to investors with assets in the hands of bankrupt and otherwise financially troubled brokerage firms.

http://www.fdic.gov/ Check the bank find function on the Federal Deposit Insurance Corporation's home page to make sure your bank is actually insured.

http://www.consumerfinance.gov/ In a first by a federal financial regulator, the Consumer Financial Protection Bureau (CFPB) will share with the public individual-level consumer complaint data received by the CFPB.

http://www.stocktransfer.com/index.cfm?action=companies. directories.escheat Escheatment offices by state from stock transfer, which is also used as a vehicle to educate shareholders about their investments and give them access to services and professionals who can assist them.

http://www.unclaimed.org/ National Association of Unclaimed Property Administrators provides a free national search to reunite you with your unclaimed property maintained by the state officials who are safeguarding it.

http://www.bloomberg.com/ Bloomberg's founding vision in 1981 was to create an information-services, news, and media company that provides business and financial professionals with the tools and data they need on a single, all-inclusive platform. The success of Bloomberg is due to the constant innovation of their products, unrivaled dedication to customer service, and the unique way in which they constantly adapt to an ever-changing marketplace.

http://online.barrons.com/ This Dow Jones Company, with its subsidiaries and network, comprises business and financial news websites read by millions of business decision-makers around the world. *Barron's* is America's premier financial magazine, renowned for its market-moving stories and in-depth reporting.

http://www.forbes.com/ Being the publishers of America's favorite lists is just one area of expertise for this huge media conglomerate. A sneak peek at some of the most popular lists Americans love to read every year are as follows: Largest Private Companies, World's Richest People, 400 Richest Americans, 100 Top Celebrities, Most Expensive Zip Codes, Most Expensive Cars to Insure, World's Best Airlines, and Best Business Schools. They are a full-service information and media provider.

http://money.cnn.com/magazines/fortune/ This CNN Money subsidiary owns *Fortune* magazine and provides a Business Leader Council, which is a market research panel that offers you the opportunity to share your views on business, personal finance, and other issues.

http://money.cnn.com/ This Time Warner company has a whole lot of high-end financial publications as well as CNN television.

http://www.crains.com/ Crain Communications is primarily a publishing company providing vital news and information to industry leaders and consumers, with over thirty titles. Each newspaper, magazine, and electronic news site has become required reading and an authoritative source in its own sector of business, trade, and consumer market.

http://www.smartmoney.com/   SmartMoney.com's customer service team is there to provide fast, friendly, and reliable service on all customer issues. Their service page is designed to help users explore and utilize SmartMoney.com tools and resources, while providing virtual customer service.

http://www.kiplinger.com/ Founded in 1920 by Kiplinger, the company developed one of the nation's first successful newsletters in modern times. The *Kiplinger Letter*, launched in 1923, remains the longest continuously published newsletter in the United States. In 1947, Kiplinger's created the nation's first personal finance magazine. Located in the heart of our nation's capital, the Kiplinger editors remain dedicated to delivering sound, unbiased advice for your family and your business in clear, concise language.

http://www.ft.com/home/us The *Financial Times* is firmly established as one of the world's leading business information brands, internationally recognized for its authoritative, accurate, and incisive news, comment, and analysis. Whether in print or online, the *Financial Times* is essential reading for the global business community.

http://www.investors.com/ *Investor's Business Daily* is a national business and financial daily newspaper that serves investors worldwide through a variety of proprietary products and services, and relevant news from the investor's perspective, as well as innovative research, investment education, efficient stock ratings and screens unavailable anywhere else. IBD differs from traditional market journalism and provides an unconventional but more research-based approach to interpreting the economy and identifying emerging stock market trends.

http://www.portfolio.com/ Portfolio.com strives to capture the intrigue, excitement, and power that attract people to the business world. The site pairs award-winning reporters with renowned photographers, videographers, and artists to bring the day's most compelling business stories to life. It's a unique vantage point for an online business site. The website says, "Rather than chase every breaking news item, we handpick the stories that will really make an impact—and go deep."

http://www.traderdaily.com/ Founder Magnus Greaves and President and Editor-in-Chief Randall Lane founded Doubledown Media as a vehicle for delivering cutting-edge professional and lifestyle content to the world of professional traders in 2004, and they have been expanding their titles ever since.

http://online.wsj.com/public/us The *Wall Street Journal*'s mission says it all ... To be the world's best provider of business content and information services across all consumer and enterprise media channels. This megamedia News Corporation asset is just one of many of this media medium's assets.

http://www.businessweek.com/ Business Week provides a very useful tool for skip tracers. With the company lookup search bar you can dig into data on more than three hundred and fifty companies—public and private—worldwide. Research over a million execs, what they make, how they intersect.

http://financialweek.com/ Financial Week is another Crain Communication media publication with an advanced search tool for looking up terms, phrases, words, and people since its inception on June 5, 2006.

http://www.investmentnews.com/ Since 1998, InvestmentNews has been delivering news and analysis essential to the business of financial advisers. Their weekly newspaper, which combines comprehensive news with accurate, independent reporting on the entire financial services industry, provides financial advisers with insight into the market unavailable in any other publication. Today, their readers have come to rely on InvestmentNews for up-to-date market information on the stories and events affecting their clients' investments, making them the leader source of news to the financial adviser community.

http://www.businesswire.com/ Business Wire is a Berkshire Hathaway company and is the leading source for press releases, photos, multimedia, and regulatory filings from companies and groups throughout the world.

http://www.reuters.com/ Thomson Reuters is the world's leading source of intelligent information for businesses and professionals. With Reuters formed 157 years ago and

Thomson formed 78 years ago, that would give them 235 years of combined experience. They combine industry expertise with innovative technology to deliver critical information to leading decision-makers in the financial, legal, tax and accounting, scientific, healthcare and media markets, powered by the world's most trusted news organization.

http://www.ap.org/ The Associated Press is the backbone of the world's information system, serving thousands of daily newspaper, radio, television, and online customers with coverage in all media and news in all formats. It is the largest and oldest news organization in the world, serving as a source of news, photos, graphics, audio, and video.

http://www.marketwatch.com/ MarketWatch is a wholly owned subsidiary of Dow Jones & Company and is a leading innovator in business news, personal finance information, real-time commentary, and investment tools and data. The company generates more than fourteen hundred headlines, stories, and market briefs a day from one hundred journalists in ten bureaus in the United States, London, and Hong Kong, in addition to operating two award-winning websites, MarketWatch. com and BigCharts.com, as well as the stock market simulation site.

http://www.mortgagedaily.com/ Founded in 1998 by a mortgage industry veteran, MortgageDaily.com has become a dominant online news publication for people in the mortgage industry. Thousands of articles written by dozens of reporters and writers chronicle the highs and lows of real estate finance. Stories about mortgage brokers, financial regulators, and other individuals associated with real estate finance are also included among the headlines. Popular topics include mortgage litigation, mortgage compliance and mortgage mergers. Other interesting subjects are originations, employment and appraisals. They also have tables rich with data are featured for mortgage originations, mortgage loans outstanding and delinquency. Other available statistics are available for mortgage-backed securities, mortgage employment and the number of mortgage firms. They have several affiliates which are TheMortgageGraveyard. com; MortgageChronicle.com; MobileMortgageNews. com; FraudBlogger.com; and CloserBlog.com.

These links are important to know and understand because your skip could be a financial professional and you need to be where he is. If you are not familiar with these links, you will be looking in the wrong place and won't find what you are looking for.

Real Estate Records

Real estate is a fertile market for skip tracers to pursue. Fraudsters still lurk within the shadows, ripping off the innocent. The following links cover frauds and real estate in general.

www.hud.gov US Department of Housing and Urban Development website to report fraud in HUD programs and operations to the HUD Inspector General Hotline.

www.usdoj.gov US Department of Justice website with a state directory of websites and press releases.

www.fbi.gov Federal Bureau of Investigation page for FBI case reports, mortgage fraud statistics, and news.

www.ftc.gov Federal Trade Commission site for mortgage fraud and identity theft investigation leading to law enforcement action.

www.fincen.gov/ The financial crimes enforcement network's mission is to enhance US national security, deter and detect criminal activity, and safeguard financial systems from abuse by promoting transparency in the United States and international financial systems.

www.federalreserveconsumerhelp.gov This website provides information on home mortgages and filing complaints from Federal Reserve Board of Governors of the Federal Reserve System.

www.theifp.org/ Institute for Fraud Prevention's mission is to globally reduce fraud and corruption.

www.ncua.gov National Credit Union Association's Fraud Hotline Report covers suspected fraud or illegal activity committed by national credit union employees, members, or officials in federally insured credit unions.

www.federalreserveconsumerhelp.gov Information on home mortgages and filing complaints from Federal

Reserve Board of Governors of the Federal Reserve System.

www.mersinc.org/ The mortgage electronic registration system is an innovative process that simplifies the way mortgage ownership and servicing rights are originated, sold, and tracked. Created by the real estate finance industry, MERS eliminates the need to prepare and record assignments when trading residential and commercial mortgage loans.

www.occ.treas.gov Office of the Comptroller of the Currency's web page to report fraud or complaints about national banks.

www.ots.treas.gov Office of Thrift Supervision will let you report fraud or register complaints about federal savings and loan associations.

www.mortgageprocessor.org/ National Association of Loan Processors is primarily educational but still has some good tools.

www.moneylaundering.com The world's leading authority on money laundering news, guidance, and analysis since 1989. It offers websites both in English and Spanish.

www.crimes-of-persuasion.com/Victims/investigation. htm This online background verification service lets you instantly access numerous public records databases for your personal investigations.

www.aicpa.org/ The American Institute of Certified Public Accountants shepherds the experts and the industries.

www.acfe.org Report fraud to the Association of Certified Fraud Examiners and get the best help from the experts.

www.fraud.org A project of the National Consumers League that focuses on fraud, including mortgage fraud and mortgage scams provided by the National Loan Auditors.

www.fraudblogger.com/ The *FraudBlogger Index* was created by *MortgageDaily.com* and utilizes mortgage fraud. They exclude investor fraud and foreclosure fraud.

www.flippingfrenzy.com/ Flipping Frenzy is your source for news, information, and commentary on real estate and mortgage fraud. Submit a news tip online. Report fraud online. Since 2005 this site has become the source for news, information, and commentary about real estate and mortgage fraud.

www.scambusters.org Research internet scams, identity theft, and urban legends.

www.scamwatch.com/ This will help you understand how to avoid Internet and money-making scams.

www.taf.org Taxpayers Against Fraud education fund is a nonprofit, public interest organization dedicated to combating fraud against the federal government through the promotion and use of the Federal False Claims Act and its qui tam provisions.

www.insurancefraud.org/ Since its founding in 1993, the coalition has worked effectively to reduce and control everyone's costs.

www.ultimateinsurancelinks.com/ Make sure the company you are using is legitimate by checking the insurance industry search and link directory.

www.pciaa.net PCI is the nation's premier insurer trade association, representing over one thousand companies that write 37.4 percent of the property casualty market. The association is also an advocate for sound public policy.

www.insurance-research.org/ The Insurance Research Council is a nonprofit division of the American Institute for Chartered Property Casualty Underwriters and the Insurance Institute of America.

www.aicpcu.org American Institute for Chartered Property Casualty Underwriters and the Insurance Institute of America and the Insurance Institute of America are independent, nonprofit organizations offering educational programs and professional certification to people in all segments of the property and liability insurance business.

www.nicb.org National insurance crime bureau was formed in 1992 from a merger between the National Automobile Theft Bureau (NATB) and the Insurance Crime Prevention Institute (ICPI), both of which were not-for-profit organizations.

www.iii.org/ Insurance information institute is improving public understanding of insurance—what it does and how it works.

www.aria.org American Risk & Insurance Association's ability to provide networking, information, and support on important insurance issues makes it a valuable organization to its members.

www.mortgagefraudblog.com/ Mortgage Fraud Blog is a premier website for news and information on mortgage fraud and real estate fraud throughout the United States.

www.stopfraud.gov/protect-mortgage.html The Financial Fraud Enforcement Task Force maintains a wide list of resources and information dedicated to helping find and report suspected cases of financial fraud.

www.identitytheftassistance.org/ ITAC, the Identity Theft Assistance Center, is the leading consumer advocate on identity fraud and the financial services industry's identity management solution center. An affiliate of The Financial Services Roundtable, ITAC is supported by the industry as a free service for our customers. The ITAC database of identity theft cases is a valuable resource for those seeking a greater understanding of the causes and consequences of identity theft. ITAC periodically conducts surveys of identity theft victims and shares information with policymakers, academics, and journalists. ITAC partners with academia on projects related to fraud and identity theft.

www.idtheftcenter.org/ Identity Theft Resource Center (ITRC) is a nonprofit, nationally respected organization dedicated exclusively to the understanding of identity theft and related issues. The ITRC provides victim and consumer support as well as public education. The ITRC also advises governmental agencies, legislators, law enforcement, and businesses about the evolving and growing problem of identity theft. They provide best in class victim assistance at no charge to consumers throughout the United States. They educate consumers, corporations, government agencies and other organizations on best practices for fraud and identity theft detection, reduction and mitigation.

www.zillow.com/ Founded in 2005, Zillow is an online real estate service dedicated to helping you get an edge in real estate by providing you with valuable tools and information.

www.trulia.com/ A new online real estate service; the search results include foreclosures—plus, pretty cool search kit tools.

www.propertyshark.com Find all the data you need for easy property research, including detailed property reports, foreclosure and "for sale" listings, comparable tools, maps, and much more.

www.streeteasy.com/ When you search for a sale or rental listing on StreetEasy, you are get the full scope of the market, custom-tailored to your exact needs. Price, location, bedrooms are just the start. We have tons of perks for the meticulous home hunter; an Advanced Search allows you to refine by price per square foot, amenities, public school zoning, commute time and much more.

www.localrealtor.com/ Browse hundreds of foreclosures, instant access to foreclosure deals, and other buyers and seller services.

www.closenow.com/ Buy or sell services with added features.

www.agentrank.com/ AgentRank is a system for ranking Realtors based on professional experience, recent home sales, endorsements from past clients, and other variables. How does your agent rank? Find out.

www.agentscoreboard.com/ Agent Scoreboard is a way for you to find great real estate agents. Agent Scoreboard allows you to search for agents in your local area and read reviews and comments posted by real people that have used their services. The scoreboard for Realtors.

www.imrealestateagent.com/ This is the largest real estate agent registry, featuring more than 1,128,821 certified agents. Please browse by state and then city. You can use the map below. They offer *free* listings. A real estate agent registry.

www.homethinking.com/ Homethinking is an online service that helps home owners choose the most remarkable neighborhood real estate agents to sell their house. They measure performance by monitoring real estate transactions to know which houses each real estate agent has sold, for how much, and how long on average it took them to do so. Homethinking shows you transactional histories of real estate agents and mortgage lenders. Realtors are ranked by their past sales and customer reviews.

www.incredibleagents.com/ IncredibleAgents.com is a real estate agent review service that helps home buyers and sellers find an Incredible Agent who can assist them in their real estate transactions. They realize consumers need to be informed when making a hiring decision about real estate agents. They will arm these consumers with more information about each agent and hopefully find the one Incredible Agent who will help them with their transaction. Check out incredible agents.

www.realtyagentsportal.com/ A portal for realty agents.

www.realtor.org/ The National Organization for Realtors (NAR) offers information and tools to help Realtors communicate the benefits of home ownership. Learn what's available to you.

www.real-estate-agent-lists.com/ Offers the most complete, accurate, and affordable Realtor lists on the Internet with the most generous usage license and satisfaction guarantee. The only limitation on the usage of our Realtor list is that you cannot resell it nor republish it for public viewing ... it is intended for marketing purposes only. We guarantee all contact information to be at least 95 percent accurate or we will immediately provide a prorated refund.

www.forclosures.com/ Some features to view are Foreclosure Lists, Foreclosure Training, Foreclosure Tools, free Forclosure Lists, How to do Foreclosure Lists, Foreclosure Consultants, State Foreclosure Listings, Affiliate Programs, and more.

www.foreclosurenet.net Get instant access to the most accurate national database of bank foreclosures and government foreclosed properties. Choose from the following: HUD, single-family homes, condos, townhomes, rental and income properties, and more.

www.homeinfomax.com/ Instant access to property information is now available for over 3,100 counties in 50 states! Residential, commercial, industrial, agricultural, land—all types of real estate records are included. Search by property address; search statewide by owner name; or search by parcel number.

www.realtor.com/ If you are you searching for property records in the United States, then you've come to the right place. At REALTOR.com, you can browse public property records for various properties across the United

States. From home values to recent selling dates and prices, you'll find everything you need here (operated by National Association of Realtors).

Collections Resources

Collecting debt is a big part of the skip tracing industry. While the two disciplines are different, both overlap. The following links will provide you with insight into the collections business, and they'll give you practical ways to track down the deadbeats.

http://www.creditandcollectionnews.com/classifieds. php This is the credit and collections industry's premier daily provider.

http://www.mycollectionjobs.com/ Whether you're looking for a career or want to know the latest news on what is going on in the debt collections industry, MyCollectionJobs.com provides the companies and individuals with the tools needed to do just that. With their many years of combined experience in the financial industry.

http://jobs.insidearm.com/home/home.cfm?site id=9007 The mission of insideARM.com is to shift the public conversation about the ARM industry in order to help creditors and collection professionals reduce risk, lawsuits, and bad press; we'd like to change consumer perception that speaking with collectors should be avoided. ARM stands for Accounts Receivable Management—also known as *debt collection*.

http://www.collectionjobs.co/ With traditional job search websites, you have to sift through hundreds or even thousands of listings to find the ones you're interested in. At CollectionJobs.com, they specialize in accounts receivable and collection jobs, linking experienced debt recovery professionals with reputable financial services companies.

http://www.jobsincredit.com/ is the UK's only jobs board dedicated to advertising roles within all areas of credit and collections, but they have an international placement department.

http://www.collectionscreditrisk.com/ Driving solutions for credit and collections personnel. This is a Source Media company.

http://columbialist.com/collection-industry-recruiting. htm The Columbia Law List with its new partnerships nationally, can now offer professional Credit & Collection Industry recruitment and placement of key personnel for collection law firms, collection agencies and creditors alike.

http://cin.jobamatic.com/a/jobs/find-jobs/q-collections Collection jobs from the Columbia List, powered by Simply Hired.

http://jobs.collectiontechnology.net/ AccountsRecovery. net and its publisher, Royal Media Group. It is the only dedicated professional network for accounts-receivable professionals. They boast more than three thousand members from internal accounts receivable departments, third-party collection agencies and other related industry professionals. Since 1995 this is the place where accounts receivable people meet online.

http://career.nacm.org/ NACM was founded in 1896 to promote good laws for sound credit, protect businesses against fraudulent debtors, improve the interchange of credit information, develop better credit practices and methods, and establish a code of ethics.

http://www.smartcredit.com/howItWorks/app-center. jsp Smart Credit is powered by Consumer Direct, which builds and markets patented or patent-pending business and consumer tools for credit, identity, and finance.

http://www.creditsesame.com/about/jobs/ Credit Sesame is one of the fastest growing start-ups in personal finance space that is revolutionizing the way people manage their credit and loans to save money. Located in Sunnyvale, CA, and backed by top-tier investors, Credit Sesame is a game-changing company with a disruptive technology and business model.

http://www.creditjobstoday.com/ CreditJobsToday. com is a database-driven career site for credit jobs and all trade credit positions. If you're looking for a credit job, collection job, or A/R job, or are just curious, you'll find a confidential place to keep your eyes open for the opportunity that best suits your needs. If you're an employer, you'll find more credit, collections, and A/R talent with résumés here than anywhere else!

http://www.careerbuilder.com/Jobs/Industry/Credit-Loan-Collections/ Career Builder is a global leader in human capital solutions. Through constant innovation, unparalleled technology, and customer care delivered at every touch point, they help match the right talent with the right opportunity more often than any other site.

http://www.recovery.gov/opportunities/pages/jobs.aspx Recovery.gov is the US government's official website that provides easy access to data related to Recovery Act spending and allows for the reporting of potential fraud, waste, and abuse.

http://www.job-applications.com/ This is the number-one online job application resource website. Complete an online job application for over one thousand companies now! If you are a skip tracer, you can apply to some of America's top employers that are hiring right now, right where you live.

http://searchnetmgt.com/links.html#career Apply online right now. Choose your zip code and your specialty and select from some of America's best employers that are hiring today.

Legal Records

One of the first and biggest cases I ever worked on was against a lawyer who became disbarred. He owed legal fees in connection with a real estate transaction to another attorney. The debt had been reduced to a judgment and now my attorney client wanted to get paid and couldn't find any accounts. After going through my step-by-step search process, I found out that my skip and his son had the same exact name. There was no junior or senior, and they both had the same middle initial. I made sure to go back and double-check every step to make sure I did not make a mistake and do the search on the wrong person. It turned out that the disbarred attorney did not have any account under his Social Security number. He only had a business checking account. This in itself is against the law because attorneys are required to have either an escrow account, interest only account IOLA, trust account, or an operating account in addition to a regular account. When they only have one account, the odds are good that commingling of funds occurred on a regular basis.

When my attorney client went to serve the bank, the information subpoena came back as "no account found." My attorney client was very upset with me, and I told him I would go back in and reverify the information. I did verify that the account he had was a business checking account under his business tax ID number and it was open and active. But the problem was that the judgment was against the cheating attorney individually and as a person and not as a business. The name on the account was Cheater Lawyer, PC. My attorney client then took my information to the local bar association, and my skip was first placed under the disciplinary action section and then eventually barred from practicing law in New York. If I were to bet, I'd say he's involved in real estate transactions and practicing an unlicensed practice of law.

Legal links are important to the skip tracer. Some hard-core intentional skips are actually attorneys who have been disbarred and are now entrepreneurs that know the laws better than most.

When some of these unethical lawyers were put out of business because they committed crimes, they found other ways of making a living. Some of those ways do not include practicing law but rather starting out another business entity that could be a means to accomplish whatever goal they had set up for themselves.

Let's elevate the bar and raise the standards. The legal industry does not just include lawyers but also academic positions; administrative and office support; contract and temporary staff; corporate counsel; in-house counsel; legal secretary; litigation support and it's support; paralegal; partner; public interest and nonprofit staff; court reporter; jury consultant; compliance specialist; e-discovery professionals; law librarian, and stenographers.

Attorneys dedicate large portions of their budget to marketing efforts, but signing new clients only happens if there is a set follow-through plan. Deals are lost when potential clients can't reach you on their time. In the competitive legal landscape, firms need to be accessible at all times in order to capture business. Customer service is the key to success in the legal world.

A law degree can open the door to a wide variety of opportunities. They also at serve the law enforcement community and all the affiliated industries, including consultants. Data still shows that with defaults of all kinds still climbing, law careers are still highly in demand.

Clearly, the legal field is full of exciting, well-paid careers with solid futures.

Avoid failure and skip trace within these valuable links for anything and everything that is strictly legal.

http://www.martindale.com/ Martindale is the premier destination for sophisticated buyers of legal services. Generations of lawyers have relied on Martindale-Hubbell as the authoritative resource for information on the worldwide legal profession. With a history spanning 140 years, the Martindale-Hubbell legal network is powered by a database of over one million lawyers and law firms in over 160 countries. Now more than ever, Martindale-Hubbell is one of the most effective ways for lawyers and law firms to promote their practices. They are a leader in the field. This is also a good site for skip tracing entrepreneurs to prospect for new business. Whenever I have a case against a deadbeat lawyer, I check here first.

http://www.lawyers.com/ Martindale-Hubbell and Lawyers.com is the most complete, trusted source for identifying qualified legal counsel.

http://www.attorneyfind.com/ AttorneyFind has been placing consumers and business owners with attorneys online for more than twenty years!

http://lawcrawler.findlaw.com/ FindLaw is a Thomson Reuters business and provides the resources to help you practice law. Access free cases and codes, connect with your peers, and leverage FindLaw's lawyer marketing solutions to stay ahead of the competition.

http://thedebtcollector.org/ Powered by Viking World Cup.

http://hg.org/ Heiros Gamos is a full-service worldwide legal directory.

http://www.duhaime.org/ Duhaime has a great legal dictionary, resources, and law magazine and daily Lawisms.

http://www.lectlaw.com/def.htm Many consider this the net's best law dictionary with thousands of definitions and explanations of legal terms, phrases, and concepts.

http://dictionary.law.com/ Law.com's legal dictionary and portal to the legal sites and publications.

http://www.alllaw.com/ All Law is the Internet's premier law portal.

http://lawcentral.com/ Law Central is the portal of legal portals.

http://www.lawyerlounge.com/legalportals/index.php Since their focus is primarily on bringing you information on using technology in your law practice, it can be helpful to be aware of other portals that may have a broader focus, so below you will find links to other popular, and information law-related websites and portals. If you find any others that are especially helpful, please pass on the information and we will add them to our list.

http://www.ilrg.com/ PublicLegal, a product of the Internet Legal Research Group. A categorized index of select websites and thousands of locally stored web pages, legal forms, and downloadable files, this site was established in 1995 to serve as a comprehensive resource of the information available on the Internet concerning law and the legal profession.

http://www.lawdepot.com/links/legal_portals.php?&a=t LawDepot.com is a full-service and internationally rated law directory and portal.

http://www.lawsmart.com/ LawSmart is wholly owned and operated by LawInfo.com, Inc. LawInfo created the LawSmart site in order to more effectively distribute legal resources online to people who are in need of quality legal information, document creation services, and qualified attorneys.

http://www.lawguru.com/ LawGuru.com was originally started in 1996 by a Los Angeles law firm and has evolved into one of the most popular legal websites on the Internet. It is offered as a free service to the entire Internet community. LawGuru.com website is owned and operated by WebSiteBroker.

http://www.law.net/roundnet.phtml Law.Net is owned and operated by TurnPike Corp. and began services in

October 1994. It is one of the earliest Internet services dedicated to and focused upon law. Since then, Law. Net has provided clients with affordable websites that promote services and bring in clients.

http://megalaw.com/ Mega Law's mission is providing an attractive, easy-to-use Internet site that gives you quick, comprehensive access to information and products that meet your professional and personal needs. Located on the cutting-edge of law and Internet technology, they depend upon the ideas, talents, and contributions of members to make the site the best possible online legal experience. Membership is free and guarantees access to future Megalaw developments and members-only content.

http://www.lawdog.com/ Lawdog is illustrated with selections from the Fair Credit Reporting Act, as amended, Fair Debt Collection Practices Act, the Equal Credit Opportunity Act (Regulation B), selected provisions of the US Bankruptcy Code. See actual product for source descriptions. Any use of this site demonstrates conclusively your election to agree to the Terms of Use. Please read them.

http://www.lawreview.org Sign up for free law review articles by e-mail. These are free services brought to you by the educational community.

http://www.lawprofessor.com/ Law Professor is a legal portal home to hundreds of legal articles and legal resources and directories. All information is *free* and available at no cost to you.

http://www.rentlaw.com/ The landlord tenant guide to check out states rent laws and other useful information.

http://www.rocketlawyer.com/ Everything you need to make it legal.

http://www.nolo.com/ Since 1971, Nolo has offered affordable, plain-English books, forms and software on a wide range of legal issues, including wills, estate planning, retirement, elder care, personal finance, taxes, housing, real estate, divorce and child custody. They also offer materials on human resources, employment, intellectual property, and starting and running a small business.

http://www.blumberg.com/ Blumberg has been serving the legal community for over 120 years with legal forms and electronic applications.

http://www.legalzoom.com/ LegalZoom was developed by expert attorneys with experience at the most prestigious law firms in the country, and the Education Center allows you to access the information you need to make informed decisions.

http://www.legalink.com/ Schedule expert court reporters and videographers—anywhere, anytime. This site is operated by Merrill Company in St. Paul that was started in 1968. Merrill has become a leading provider of outsourced document management, branded marketing services and other information management solutions to targeted vertical markets. Their solutions enable clients to create, access, control, analyze and communicate critical information for strategy, marketing and regulatory compliance Delivered through a mix of proprietary technologies, industry specific processes and outsourced services. Their solutions maximize both value and ease of use for their customers.

http://www.law.com/jsp/nlj/index.jsp The National Law Journal provides timely legal information of national importance to attorneys that other publications don't.

http://experts.com/ Since 1994, Experts.com has been providing millions of users worldwide with access to the information and expertise that they need. As one of the nation's most established and premier Internet registries, they serve as a "who's who" of experts at the top of their respective fields. Listed experts include authors, consultants, engineers, physicians, professors, scientists, specialists, and more. The registry has been a resource to attorneys, businesses, reporters, insurance companies, judges, librarians, the media, and countless others. Be there!

http://www.abanet.org/tech/ltrc/lawlink/home.html American Bar Association's Lawlink: The Legal Research Jumpstation.

http://www.abanet.org/barserv/stlobar.html The American Bar Association lets you view contact information for the state and local bars therein.

http://www.americanbar.org/aba.html The American Bar Association is the largest voluntary professional association in the world. With nearly four hundred thousand members, the ABA provides law school accreditation, continuing legal education, information about the law, programs to assist lawyers and judges in their work, and initiatives to improve the legal system for the public. Their mission is to serve equally their members, their profession and the public by defending liberty and delivering justice as the national representative of the legal profession.

http://www.nationalboardofcollectionattorneys.com/ NBCA's mission is to help elevate the moral standards and practices of collection attorneys and their debt collectors by providing an exclusive membership program whereby all members of NBCA must strictly adhere to a best practices platform in the collection of debt. NBCA prequalifies and prescreens all potential collection attorney members utilizing requirement standards, an informative application process and insightful due diligence.

http://www.ccaacollect.com/ The CCAA was established in 1972 to improve the quality and reputation of the commercial collection industry. It is part of the Commercial Law League of America (CLLA), the oldest creditors' rights organization in the country, founded in 1895.

http://www.attorneysmarket.biz/ A plethora of legal necessities for attorneys.

Skip Tracing Career Resources

When planning your career as a skip tracer, you will need to play "catch me if you can." Here are some of the best places to start online. Try these tried-and-true resources that are sure to put you in the right path.

http://attorneyjobs.com/ AttorneyJobs.com, part of Thomson Reuters, is the Nation's number-one job site exclusively for attorneys, containing thousands of jobs nationwide and abroad covering legal and law-related job opportunities in law firms; corporations; public interest/advocacy groups; Federal, state, and local governments; Federal, state, and local courts; legal service organizations; international organizations; colleges and universities; as well as information about RFPs/appointments and fellowships.

http://www.lawyerintl.com/legal-jobs.php Today's legal market is thriving, and lucrative job opportunities within it extend far beyond those available to attorneys and paralegals. Careers based on using technology, medicine and psychology in a legal context are exploding in popularity, and jobs in the legal field are no longer limited to those who have passed the bar. Whether you're interested in nursing, writing or computers, there's likely a job in the legal sphere that you'd be perfect for. Check out this list of the hottest legal careers and see what could be in store for you. And much more.

http://jobs.lawbulletin.com/ If you're looking for a job in a law firm or corporate law environment, this site contains attorney jobs, paralegal jobs, legal secretary jobs, law/

docket clerk, and legal administrator job postings plus many other legal resources to help your career. All job ads are updated weekdays at 3:30 p.m. This service is powered by Law Bulletin from Chicago's daily law bulletin.

http://lawyerist.com/ Lawyerist is the number-one law practice blog. They write about marketing, practice management, career development, and more. It is a forum for lawyers and law students to discuss law practice, lawyering, technology, legal marketing, law school, and anything else.

http://www.lawjobs.com/ This site is powered by www.law.com and it would be hard to go wrong with them. This is the place where information and opportunity meet. As one of the most well-known and respected business franchises in the global legal services industry.

http://www.legalstaff.com/ Your destination for exciting legal job opportunities and the best resource for qualified candidates within the legal industry.

http://legal.jobs.net/ Powered by www.jobs.com, they offer placement service nationwide.

http://www.legal-jobs.com/ Filcro Legal Staffing is one of New York City's leading recruitment firms specializing in the identification of legal support and legal administrative staff. The firm's clients include law firms and major corporations that require the utmost care in identifying the proper employees. Firms and candidates that enjoy the services offered experience one the lowest turnover rates in the legal industry. Stability and professionalism are required within every legal environment and Filcro Legal Staffing offers both. Please feel free to view the various types of legal jobs in New York City listed below.

http://www.ihirelegal.com/ The team of Job Search Agents at iHireLegal.com provides you with advice and insights that have proven successful for the thousands of people that iHireLegal.com has helped monthly since 1999. iHireLegal.com provides a variety of services to help you get hired—even in this economy—including customizable online profiles, résumé rewrites, and job alerts that make your job search easier. Bottom line: They're the hiring experts, so you don't have to be.

https://www.theladders.com/ TheLadders brings you real, salaried jobs across every industry and sector that only match your goals. You can connect with over twelve thousand recruiters confidentially, and improve your résumé with our in-house certified experts. If you're looking for your next career move, you won't find a more comprehensive resource anywhere.

http://www.streetlaw.com/ Streetlaw.com is the new and exciting website for Street Law teachers and students. Each button on this site is the gateway to great stuff. Cases and Resources contains hundreds of links to sites organized to coordinate with the contents of the Street Law text, many with activities. Supersites links you to the best all-around law-related sites on the web. These buttons have been specially constructed to withstand billions of clicks because we know you will use them over and over again.

http://www.merrillcorp.com/career-opportunities 113. Merrill Corporation Receives Multiple Awards in National Law Journal Reader Survey.

http://thedebtcollector.org/job-board.htm Powered by Viking World Cup.

http://www.edebtcollector.org/ The difference between eDebtCollector and other collection directories is very simple, we have the best search engine optimization specialist in the Collection Industry at the helm and we provide exclusive listings for all collection agencies interested in branding their firm names and receiving high end web exposure.

http://www.collectionworld.org/ CollectionWorld.org is a free directory for all companies associated with the Collection Industry, whether you are a collection attorney, skip tracer, payment processor, etc., we provide valuable free exposure to promote your brand! Get your free listing today.

http://www.attorneyscollect.org/ Another great Viking World Cup resource.

http://www.lawfirmjobs.us/ Their job board is dedicated to providing the latest job postings for attorneys, paralegals, legal assistant's law clerks, and legal secretaries in order to fill the staffing requirements of law firms throughout the

United States. LawFirmJobs.US is one of the best online resources available for finding a law firm job or for posting one on our extensive job board. Our job board is linked to more than five thousand other job-related websites on the Internet, and it has literally thousands of law firm jobs available for viewing on a local, regional, or national basis. Please peruse our comprehensive employment database or post a job for massive exposure across the Internet.

http://www.justice.gov/careers/legal/ The Department of Justice offers a broad range of opportunities for experienced attorneys to work on many significant and complex issues that face our nation. Our lawyers work in virtually every area of legal practice. Any attorney who is an active member of the bar of any US jurisdiction and has at least one year post-JD legal or other relevant experience is eligible to apply for any experienced attorney position.

Other Useful Links

This link section is about anything that can be useful and will enhance your functionality. Sometimes the most interesting stuff is hiding in plain sight. With the right awareness and friendly web tools, you can find what you are looking for. Sometimes it is as simple as choosing the best search for your information needs. With some ingenuity and practice, your performance will get better.

http://www.freeadvice.com/ Free advice ... can't beat the price. FreeAdvice.com also has benefited from advice from members of its distinguished former Editorial

Advisory Board comprised of distinguished attorneys, including law school deans and law professors, consumer advocates, former senior Government officials, senior partners at several of America's leading law firms and senior counsel in leading corporate law departments.

http://www.weddingchannel.com/ Search for weddings by name and state.

http://www.wa-wd.com/ Who's alive and who's dead, by categories, including recent deaths, new listings, performers, politicians, athletes, and more.

http://www.arrangeonline.com/ View obituaries by city and state. The National Obituary Archive is the world's largest repository of obituaries and death records with more than fifty-five million individual entries on file. Visitors may search the archive freely to learn about the deaths of friends or family or to explore relationships when building family trees or doing genealogical research.

http://www.interment.net/ Search this free online library of cemetery records from thousands of cemeteries across the world, for historical and genealogy research. Search and browse cemetery burial records from thousands of cemeteries across the world.

http:www.degreeverify.com The National Student Clearinghouse is the nation's #1 source for education verification offering the largest online collection of enrollment and degree data.

http://www.studentclearinghouse.org/ The National Student Clearinghouse, a nonprofit organization, is the nation's trusted source for student degree and enrollment verification for verification reporting solutions.

http://www.directoryofschools.com/ Find online schools, accredited online degrees online colleges, on-campus degree programs, online certificates, online courses and online training; plus all of our online degree programs offer job placement opportunities for graduates. Take control and be empowered.

http://www.accredibase.com/ To help employers, educators and background screening companies secure only the best candidates with bona fide qualifications This searchable global database brings together powerful information on bogus institutions from a variety of sources.

http://www.degreeinfo.com/content/ The oldest and largest online community for distance/online learning today.

http://www.braintrack.com/ This is the web's most complete directory for university and college searches. Operating since 1996, they list over ten thousand higher education institutions in 194 countries, and the list is continually updated with new resources for education. Not a corporate search, but know what resources are available to you.

http://www.npr.org/ National Public Radio is a partner in PBS, Public Broadcasting Service. If your skip is a guest speaker on one of these shows, you can do a name search for shows.

http://publicradiofan.com/ PublicRadioFan.com features schedule listings for thousands of public radio stations and programs around the world. Follow the audio links to hear your favorite programs and discover new ones.

http://www.radio-locator.com/ The most comprehensive radio station search engine on the Internet. We have links to over ten thousand radio station web pages and over 2,500 audio streams from radio stations in the United States and around the world.

http://www.birthdatabase.com/ The birthday data is obtained from public records and available to anyone with a simple knowledge of public record access and is part of bored.com.

http://www.anybirthday.com/ Anybirthday.com was first established in 1999 as an easy way to look up and be reminded of the birth dates of people that are important in your life via a database of over 135 million birth records.

http://www.birthdate.com/ Keep track of birthdays and see who's on.

http://www.namepedia.org/ Namepedia is the world's largest information platform and community about personal names. Data is collected about names of all languages and cultures, in all scripts, with a focus on the Latin alphabet.

http://namechk.com/ Check to see if your desired username or vanity URL is still available at dozens of popular social networking and social bookmarking websites. Promote your brand consistently by registering a username that is still available on the majority of the most popular sites.

http://www.behindthename.com/ Names. Everyone has one, most people have a vague idea what their own means, but few give them much more thought. The study of names is called onomastics, a field which touches on linguistics, history, anthropology, psychology, sociology, philology, and much more. When people refer to the "meaning of a name," they are most likely referring to the etymology, which is the original literal meaning. This website looks at the etymology and history of all types of given names. The etymology and history of first names.

http://www.adoption.com/ Adoption.com is committed to helping as many children as possible find loving, permanent homes. They also provide critical information at the decision-making moment to women facing crisis pregnancies. They assist adoptees and birthparents to find birth families, and they help hopeful adoptive parents make adoption dreams come true. They are especially committed to helping special needs children in the United States and around the world, who otherwise wouldn't be able to find families.

http://www.gale.cengage.com/ The encyclopedia of encyclopedias. They offer free trails.

http://www.refdesk.com/ One of the most comprehensive reference tools on the Internet. The ICU of the Internet.

http://www.encyclopedia.com/ Encyclopedia.com has more than one hundred trusted sources including encyclopedias, dictionaries, and thesauruses with facts, definitions, biographies, synonyms, pronunciation keys, word origins, and abbreviations.

http://directoryofdirectories.in/ Directoryofdirectories.in is a free resource which provides listing of topic-based web directories. If you manage a web directory or know someone who does, then you are invited to submit your website directory to this listing. They are trying to approve all directories within first forty-eight hours.

http://www.reputation.com/ People are posting new content on the Internet every day. Keep tabs on your reputation with their *free* Internet monitoring service. Everyone should be able to control his or her own online reputation, and all the private data that includes.

http://www.switchboard.com/ Another search directory.

http://computer.howstuffworks.com How Stuff Works lets you search for a large range of stuff.

http://www.infoplease.com/ All the info you need.

http://www.findology.com/ Get accurate, real-time salary reports based on your job title, location, education, skills, and experience.

http://www.salary.com/ What we can earn and how we earn it plays a dominant role in our lives. It is a measure of where we are in our careers—our successes and our struggles. But more importantly, the money we earn helps us live the life we seek. Salary.com is devoted to delivering accurate and credible salary calculations and salary-related advice. But they also understand that your salary and earning potential empowers you to make pivotal life decisions—like picking a college, or buying a home or retiring early. Salary.com is more than just salary information, its advice on making life's decisions. The Salary Wizard and other salary evaluation tools are a definite plus.

http://www.canada411.ca/ Find a person or a business in Canada.

http://www.noodletools.com/debbie/literacies/information/5locate/adviceengine.html Choose the best search strategies for your information needs.

http://images.info.com/ Find images and photos. The smartest image search on the web.

www.picsearch.com/ Find your pictures at Picsearch.com! They have billions of indexed images in our directory, and it continually expands.

http://www.search.com/images Search does more than search for images.

www.annualcreditreport.com Get your free credit report every year.

www.freecreditreport.com Get your free credit report with your credit score.

http://earth.google.com/ Free Google.earth download.

Secretary of State Links

The Secretary of State's Government Records Inquiry System provides you easy access to public information maintained by the Secretary of State's office in electronic format. The website for each corresponding state or territory is listed as follows:

Alabama:

http://arc-sos.state.al.us/CGI/CORPNAME.MBR/INPUT

Alaska:

http://commerce.alaska.gov/CBP/Main/CBPLSearch.aspx?mode=Corp

Arizona:

http://starpas.azcc.gov/scripts/cgiip.exe/WService=wsbroker1/main.p

Arkansas:

http://www.sos.arkansas.gov/BCS/Pages/default.aspx

California:

http://kepler.sos.ca.gov/

Colorado:

http://www.sos.state.co.us/

Connecticut:

http://www.concord-sots.ct.gov/CONCORD/online?sn=PublicInquiry&eid=9740

Delaware:

https://delecorp.delaware.gov/tin/GINameSearch.jsp

District of Columbia:

https://corp.dcra.dc.gov/Account.aspx/LogOn?ReturnUrl=%2f

Florida:

http://www.sunbiz.org/search.html

Georgia:

http://corp.sos.state.ga.us/corp/soskb/CSearch.asp

Hawaii:

http://hbe.ehawaii.gov/documents/search.html;jsessionid=9D2A97B1D257FCB5EBFE1B9486C6AC92.liona

Idaho:

http://www.accessidaho.org/public/sos/corp/search.html?SearchFormstep=crit

Illinois:

http://www.ilsos.gov/corporatellc/

Indiana:

https://secure.in.gov/sos/online_corps/name_search.aspx

Iowa:

http://sos.iowa.gov/search/business/(S(mn0qabrp1cag1kjt0xv11g55))/search.aspx

Kansas:

https://www.kansas.gov/bess/flow/main;jsessionid=21DB7865D7A4FBB9EFC97003754A060D.aptcs03-inst0?execution=e1s1

Kentucky:

https://app.sos.ky.gov/ftsearch/

Louisiana:

http://www.sos.la.gov/tabid/819/Default.aspx

Maine:

https://icrs.informe.org/nei-sos-icrs/ICRS

Maryland:

http://sdatcert3.resiusa.org/UCC-Charter/CharterSearch_f.aspx

Massachusetts:

http://corp.sec.state.ma.us/corp/corpsearch/corpsearchinput.asp

Michigan:

http://www.dleg.state.mi.us/bcs_corp/sr_corp.asp

Minnesota:

http://da.sos.state.mn.us/minnesota/corp_inquiry-find.asp?:Norder_item_type_id=10&sm=7

Mississippi:

https://business.sos.state.ms.us/corp/soskb/csearch.asp

Missouri:

https://www.sos.mo.gov/BusinessEntity/soskb/csearch.asp

Montana:

https://app.mt.gov/bes/

Nebraska:

https://www.nebraska.gov/sos/corp/corpsearch.cgi?nav=search

Nevada:

http://nvsos.gov/sosentitysearch/

New Hampshire:

https://www.sos.nh.gov/corporate/soskb/csearch.asp

New Jersey:

https://www.njportal.com/DOR/businessrecords/EntityDocs/BusinessStatCopies.aspx

New Mexico:

http://web.prc.newmexico.gov/Corplookup/(S(sqhmq0oedcsnqziw4kl3jy5u))/CorpSearch.aspx

New York:

http://www.dos.ny.gov/corps/bus_entity_search

North Carolina:

http://www.secretary.state.nc.us/corporations/csearch.aspx

North Dakota:

https://apps.nd.gov/sc/busnsrch/busnSearch.htm

Ohio:

http://www2.sos.state.oh.us/pls/bsqry/f?p=100:1:1925865968984201

Oklahoma:

https://www.sos.ok.gov/corp/corpInquiryFind.aspx

Oregon:

http://egov.sos.state.or.us/br/pkg_web_name_srch_inq.login

Pennsylvania:

https://www.corporations.state.pa.us/corp/soskb/csearch.asp?corpsNav=%7C

Puerto Rico:

https://prcorpfiling.f1hst.com/CorporationSearch.aspx

Rhode Island:

http://ucc.state.ri.us/CorpSearch/CorpSearchInput.asp

South Carolina:

http://www.scsos.com/Search%20Business%20Filings

South Dakota:

http://sdsos.gov/Business/Search.aspx

Tennessee:

http://tnbear.tn.gov/ECommerce/FilingSearch.aspx

Texas:

https://ourcpa.cpa.state.tx.us/coa/Index.html

Utah:

http://www.utah.gov/services/business.html?type=citizen

Vermont:

http://www.sec.state.vt.us/seek/corpseek.htm

Virginia:

https://sccefile.scc.virginia.gov/Find/Business

Washington:

http://www.sos.wa.gov/corps/corps_search.aspx

West Virginia:

http://apps.sos.wv.gov/business/corporations/

Wisconsin:

https://www.wdfi.org/apps/CorpSearch/Search.aspx?

Wyoming:

https://wyobiz.wy.gov/Business/DefaultBD.aspx

> *We are handicapped by what we think we can't do.*
>
> *—Mark Twain*

Chapter 10
Tracking Social Security Numbers

The first three digits of the Social Security number will determine which state the subject is from. Here is a listing of all the digit combinations and their corresponding states or territories:

001-003 New Hampshire

004-007 Maine

008-009 Vermont

010-034 Massachusetts

035-039 Rhode Island

040-049 Connecticut

050–134 New York

135–158 New Jersey

159–211 Pennsylvania

212–220 Maryland

221–222 Delaware

223–231 Virginia

232–236 West Virginia

237–246 North Carolina

247–251 South Carolina

252–260 Georgia

261–267 Florida

268–302 Ohio

303–317 Indiana

318–361 Illinois

362–386 Michigan

387–399 Wisconsin

400–407 Kentucky

408–415 Tennessee

416–424 Alabama

425–428 Mississippi

429–432 Arkansas

433–439 Louisiana

440–448 Oklahoma

449–467 Texas

468–477 Minnesota

478–485 Iowa

486–500 Missouri

501–502 North Dakota

503–504 South Dakota

505–508 Nebraska

509–515 Kansas

516–517 Montana

518–519 Idaho

520   Wyoming

521–524 Colorado

525, 585 New Mexico

526–527 Arizona

528–529 Utah

530   Nevada

531–539 Washington

540–544 Oregon

545–573 California

574   Alaska

575–576 Hawaii

577–579 District of Columbia

580   Virgin Islands

581–584 Puerto Rico, Guam, American Samoa, Philippine Islands

586   Guam, American Samoa, Mariana Islands, Philippine Islands

588   Mississippi

589–595 Florida

596–599 Puerto Rico

600–601 Arizona

602–626 California

627–645 Texas

646–647 Utah

648–649 New Mexico

Appendix A
My Services

My main business is skip tracing and locating assets, but I do a lot of teaching and training as well. Presenting seminars is one of the most rewarding pursuits of my career. I have also spent a great deal of time making my company website truly useful to visitors. For example, we have an incredible links page.

Check it out: http://www.searchnetmgt.com/links.html

It is a list of new and improved *free links* with web directories and search engines that think and can be used as a legal reference tool, with specific tips and instructions for obtaining the greatest amount of information from various sources, such as city clerks, public libraries, tax assessing offices, county clerks, post offices, chamber of commerce offices, sheriff's departments, motor vehicle departments, driver's license departments, Secretary of State offices, vital record departments, neighbors, city directories, credit bureau reports, same last names, cross reference directories, friends and relatives, military data, same line of work, creditors, Internet sites, and more. Use these as a bookmark and label them "Tricks of the Trade" for future reference.

The screen shot below shows how I organize my most-visited links.

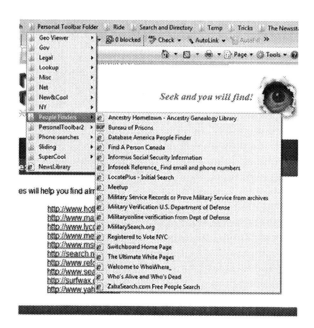

Would you like to find out more about training? Do you have a question that is not addressed in this book? You can e-mail me at <u>susan@searchnetmgt.com</u>, or you can write to me at Search-Net Management Corp, 527 Third Ave. Suite 301, New York, NY 10016. You may also call our number, (212) 447-5913. I can assure you a speedy response.

Appendix B
Postjudgment Interest Rates

Interest is allowed on most judgments entered in the federal courts from the date of judgment until paid. The calculation of postjudgment interest is much more complex than it may first appear due to the varying methods of computation from location to location. For example, in Kentucky, postjudgment interest is compounded annually on the anniversary of the judgment date, while in Oklahoma, postjudgment interest is compounded annually on the first day of January, regardless of the judgment date. The processes get tricky, and I recommend using a tool like an interest calculator that will calculate the amount for you. This can be found at http://postjudgmentinterest.com/.

State	Postjudgment Interest Rate
Alabama	12% or 10.5% unless contract calls for less
Arizona	10% unless contract calls for different rate

Arkansas	10% unless contract calls for less
California	10%
Colorado	8% unless contract calls for different rate
Connecticut	8% unless contract calls for less
Delaware	0.5% above the Federal Reserve discount rate unless contract calls for less
District of Columbia	17.5%
Florida	12% unless contract calls for less
Georgia	12% unless contract calls for different rate
Hawaii	10%
Idaho	5% above weekly average yield on T-bills
Illinois	9%
Indiana	10% unless contract calls for less
Iowa	10% unless contract calls for less
Kansas	10% unless contract calls for less
Kentucky	12% unless contract calls for less
Louisiana	Average prime rate given by 5 major banks to their most favored corporate clients on 10/1 of each year unless contract calls for less
Maine	15% for judgments under $30,000
Maryland	10% unless contract calls for different rate
Massachusetts	6% unless contract calls for different rate
Michigan	12% unless contract calls for different rate; not to exceed 13%

Minnesota	Tied to one-year T-bill; not to be lower than 13%
Mississippi	Rate stated in contract; if silent, rate is then set by judge
Missouri	9%
Montana	10%
Nebraska	Tied to one-year T-bill unless contract calls for less
Nevada	2% over the prime rate in the largest bank in Nevada on 1/1 or 7/1 preceding the judgment
New Hampshire	10%
New Jersey	8% unless contract calls for different rate
New Mexico	15% unless contract calls for different rate
New York	9%
North Carolina	12%
North Dakota	12%
Ohio	10%
Oklahoma	4% over average T-bill for preceding year
Oregon	9%
Pennsylvania	6%
Rhode Island	12%
South Carolina	14%
South Dakota	12%
Tennessee	10%
Texas	18% unless contract calls for lower rate
Utah	12% unless contract calls for different rate

Vermont	12%
Virginia	8% unless judge awards different rate
Washington	12%, or 4% above 26-week T-bill, whichever is higher; if contract calls for different rate, that rate governs as long as judgment so states
West Virginia	6% unless contract calls for different rate; not to exceed 8%
Wisconsin	12%
Wyoming	10% unless contract calls for different rate

Appendix C
Fair Debt Collection Practices Act

This law is probably the single most important law for the skip tracer directly. It was designed to protect consumers from abusive debt collectors. This law is straightforward and fair. Debt collectors simply can't hound debtors, lie to them, misrepresent themselves or the debt, and must treat the debtor with respect. You do not want to fall prey to breaking this law. A recap once again of what you can't do is as follows:

- Call the debtor before 8:00 a.m. or after 9:00 p.m.

- Contact the debtor in a harassing or abusive manner

- Call the debtor at his or her work if the employer does not allow it

- Contact the debtor if he or she has retained an attorney

- Use abusive, vulgar, or profane language

- Misrepresent the debt amount

- Misrepresent themselves as a lawyer or law enforcement officer

- Contact a third party, other than the debtor's spouse or attorney

- Threaten legal action that is not actually intended

THE FAIR DEBT COLLECTION PRACTICES ACT as amended by Pub. L. 109-351, §§ 801-02, 120 Stat. 1966 (2006).

As a public service, the staff of the Federal Trade Commission (FTC) has prepared the following complete text of the Fair Debt Collection Practices Act (FDCPA), 15 U.S.C. §§ 1692-1692p. Please note that the format of the text differs in minor ways from the U.S. Code and West's U.S. Code Annotated. For example, this version uses FDCPA section numbers in the headings. In addition, the relevant U.S. Code citation is included with each section heading. Although the staff has made every effort to transcribe the statutory material accurately, this compendium is intended as a convenience for the public and not a substitute for the text in the U.S. Code.

Table of Contents § 801 Short title § 802 Congressional findings and declaration of purpose § 803 Definitions § 804 Acquisition of location information § 805 Communication in connection with debt collection § 806 Harassment or abuse § 807 False or misleading representations § 808 Unfair practices § 809 Validation of debts § 810 Multiple debts § 811 Legal actions by debt collectors § 812 Furnishing certain deceptive forms § 813 Civil liability § 814 Administrative enforcement § 815 Reports to Congress by the Commission § 816 Relation to State laws § 817 Exemption for State regulation § 818 Exception for certain bad check enforcement programs operated by private entities § 819 Effective date.

§ 801. Short Title

This title may be cited as the "Fair Debt Collection Practices Act."

§ 802. Congressional findings and declaration of purpose

(a) There is abundant evidence of the use of abusive, deceptive, and unfair debt collection practices by many debt collectors. Abusive debt collection practices contribute to the number of personal bankruptcies, to marital instability, to the loss of jobs, and to invasions of individual privacy.

(b) Existing laws and procedures for redressing these injuries are inadequate to protect consumers.

(c) Means other than misrepresentation or other abusive debt collection practices are available for the effective collection of debts.

(d) Abusive debt collection practices are carried on to a substantial extent in interstate commerce and through means and instrumentalities of such commerce. Even where abusive debt collection practices are purely intrastate in character, they nevertheless directly affect interstate commerce.

(e) It is the purpose of this title to eliminate abusive debt collection practices by debt collectors, to insure that those debt collectors who refrain from using abusive debt collection practices are not competitively disadvantaged, and to promote consistent State action to protect consumers against debt collection abuses.

§ 803. Definitions

As used in this title—

(1) The term "Commission" means the Federal Trade Commission.

(2) The term "communication" means the conveying of information regarding a debt directly or indirectly to any person through any medium.

(3) The term "consumer" means any natural person obligated or allegedly obligated to pay any debt.

(4) The term "creditor" means any person who offers or extends credit creating a debt or to whom a debt is owed, but such term does not include any person to the extent that he receives an assignment or transfer of a debt in default solely for the purpose of facilitating collection of such debt for another.

(5) The term "debt" means any obligation or alleged obligation of a consumer to pay money arising out of a transaction in which the money, property, insurance or services which are the subject of the transaction are primarily for personal, family, or household purposes, whether or not such obligation has been reduced to judgment.

(6) The term "debt collector" means any person who uses any instrumentality of interstate commerce or the mails in any business the principal purpose of which is the collection of any debts, or who regularly collects or attempts to collect, directly or indirectly, debts owed or due or asserted to be owed or due another. Notwithstanding the exclusion provided by clause (F) of the last sentence of this paragraph, the term includes any creditor who, in the process of collecting his own debts, uses any

name other than his own which would indicate that a third person is collecting or attempting to collect such debts. For the purpose of section 808(6), such term also includes any person who uses any instrumentality of interstate commerce or the mails in any business the principal purpose of which is the enforcement of security interests. The term does not include—

(A) any officer or employee of a creditor while, in the name of the creditor, collecting debts for such creditor;

(B) any person while acting as a debt collector for another person, both of whom are related by common ownership or affiliated by corporate control, if the person acting as a debt collector does so only for persons to whom it is so related or affiliated and if the principal business of such person is not the collection of debts;

(C) any officer or employee of the United States or any State to the extent that collecting or attempting to collect any debt is in the performance of his official duties;

(D) any person while serving or attempting to serve legal process on any other person in connection with the judicial enforcement of any debt;

(E) any nonprofit organization which, at the request of consumers, performs bona fide consumer credit counseling and assists consumers in the liquidation of their debts by receiving payments from such consumers and distributing such amounts to creditors; and

(F) any person collecting or attempting to collect any debt owed or due or asserted to be owed or due another to the extent such activity

(i) is incidental to a bona fide fiduciary obligation or a bona fide escrow arrangement;

(ii) concerns a debt which was originated by such person;

(iii) concerns a debt which was not in default at the time it was obtained by such person;

Or

(iv) concerns a debt obtained by such person as a secured party in a commercial credit transaction involving the creditor.

(7) The term "location information" means a consumer's place of abode and his telephone number at such place, or his place of employment.

(8) The term "State" means any State, territory, or possession of the United States, the District of Columbia, the Commonwealth of Puerto Rico, or any political subdivision of any of the foregoing.

§ 804. Acquisition of location information

Any debt collector communicating with any person other than the consumer for the purpose of acquiring location information about the consumer shall—

(1) identify himself, state that he is confirming or correcting location information concerning the consumer, and, only if expressly requested, identify his employer;

(2) not state that such consumer owes any debt;

(3) not communicate with any such person more than once unless requested to do so by such person or unless the debt collector reasonably believes that the earlier response of such person is erroneous or incomplete and that such person now has correct or complete location information;

(4) not communicate by post card;

(5) not use any language or symbol on any envelope or in the contents of any communication effected by the mails or telegram that indicates that the debt collector is in the debt collection business or

that the communication relates to the collection of a debt; and

(6) after the debt collector knows the consumer is represented by an attorney with regard to the subject debt and has knowledge of, or can readily ascertain, such attorney's name and address, not communicate with any person other than that attorney, unless the attorney fails to respond within a reasonable period of time to the communication from the debt collector.

§ 805. Communication in connection with debt collection

(a) COMMUNICATION WITH THE CONSUMER GENERALLY. Without the prior consent of the consumer given directly to the debt collector or the express permission of a court of competent jurisdiction, a debt collector may not communicate with a consumer in connection with the collection of any debt—

(1) at any unusual time or place or a time or place known or which should be known to be inconvenient to the consumer. In the absence of knowledge of circumstances to the contrary, a debt collector shall assume that the convenient time for communicating with a consumer is after 8 o'clock antimeridian and before 9 o'clock postmeridian, local time at the consumer's location;

(2) if the debt collector knows the consumer is represented by an attorney with respect to such debt and has knowledge of, or can readily ascertain, such attorney's name and address, unless the attorney fails to respond within a reasonable period of time to a communication from the debt collector or unless the attorney consents to direct communication with the consumer; or

(3) at the consumer's place of employment if the debt collector knows or has reason to know that the consumer's employer prohibits the consumer from receiving such communication.

(b) COMMUNICATION WITH THIRD PARTIES. Except as provided in section 804, without the prior consent of the consumer given directly to the debt collector, or the express permission of a court of competent jurisdiction, or as reasonably necessary to effectuate a postjudgment judicial remedy, a debt collector may not communicate, in connection with the collection of any debt, with any person other than a consumer, his attorney, a consumer reporting agency if otherwise permitted by law, the creditor, the attorney of the creditor, or the attorney of the debt collector.

(c) CEASING COMMUNICATION. If a consumer notifies a debt collector in writing that the consumer refuses to pay a debt or that the consumer wishes the debt collector to cease further communication with the consumer, the debt collector shall not communicate further with the consumer with respect to such debt, except—

(1) to advise the consumer that the debt collector's further efforts are being terminated;

(2) to notify the consumer that the debt collector or creditor may invoke specified remedies which are ordinarily invoked by such debt collector or creditor; or

(3) where applicable, to notify the consumer that the debt collector or creditor intends to invoke a specified remedy. If such notice from the consumer is made by mail, notification shall be complete upon receipt.

(d) For the purpose of this section, the term "consumer" includes the consumer's spouse, parent (if the consumer is a minor), guardian, executor, or administrator.

§ 806. Harassment or abuse

A debt collector may not engage in any conduct the natural consequence of which is to harass, oppress, or abuse any person in connection with the collection of a debt. Without limiting the general application of the foregoing, the following conduct is a violation of this section:

(1) The use or threat of use of violence or other criminal means to harm the physical person, reputation, or property of any person.

(2) The use of obscene or profane language or language the natural consequence of which is to abuse the hearer or reader.

(3) The publication of a list of consumers who allegedly refuse to pay debts, except to a consumer reporting agency or to persons meeting the requirements of section 603(f) or 604(3) [section 604(3) has been renumbered as section 604(a)(3).15 USC 1692d] of this Act.

(4) The advertisement for sale of any debt to coerce payment of the debt.

(5) Causing a telephone to ring or engaging any person in telephone conversation repeatedly or continuously with intent to annoy, abuse, or harass any person at the called number.

(6) Except as provided in section 804, the placement of telephone calls without meaningful disclosure of the caller's identity.

§ 807. False or misleading representations

A debt collector may not use any false, deceptive, or misleading representation or means in connection with the collection of any debt. Without limiting the general application of the foregoing, the following conduct is a violation of this section:

(1) The false representation or implication that the debt collector is vouched for, bonded by, or affiliated with the United States or any State, including the use of any badge, uniform, or facsimile thereof.

(2) The false representation of—

    (A) the character, amount, or legal status of any debt; or

    (B) any services rendered or compensation which may be lawfully received by any debt collector for the collection of a debt.

(3) The false representation or implication that any individual is an attorney or that any communication is from an attorney.

(4) The representation or implication that nonpayment of any debt will result in the arrest or imprisonment of any person or the seizure, garnishment, attachment, or sale of any property or wages of any person unless such action is lawful and the debt collector or creditor intends to take such action.

(5) The threat to take any action that cannot legally be taken or that is not intended to be taken.

(6) The false representation or implication that a sale, referral, or other transfer of any interest in a debt shall cause the consumer to—

(A) lose any claim or defense to payment of the debt; or

(B) become subject to any practice prohibited by this title.

(7) The false representation or implication that the consumer committed any crime or other conduct in order to disgrace the consumer.

(8) Communicating or threatening to communicate to any person credit information which is known or which should be known to be false, including the failure to communicate that a disputed debt is disputed.

(9) The use or distribution of any written communication which simulates or is falsely represented to be a document authorized, issued, or approved by any court, official, or agency of the United States or any State, or which creates a false impression as to its source, authorization, or approval.

(10) The use of any false representation or deceptive means to collect or attempt to collect any debt or to obtain information concerning a consumer.

(11) The failure to disclose in the initial written communication with the consumer and, in addition, if the initial communication with the consumer is oral, in that initial oral communication, that the debt collector is attempting to collect a debt and that any information obtained will be used for that purpose, and the failure to disclose in subsequent communications that the communication is from a debt collector, except that this paragraph shall not apply to a formal pleading made in connection with a legal action.

(12) The false representation or implication that accounts have been turned over to innocent purchasers for value.

(13) The false representation or implication that documents are legal process.

(14) The use of any business, company, or organization name other than the true name of the debt collector's business, company, or organization.

(15) The false representation or implication that documents are not legal process forms or do not require action by the consumer.

(16) The false representation or implication that a debt collector operates or is employed by a consumer reporting agency as defined by section 603(f) of this Act.

§ 808. Unfair practices

A debt collector may not use unfair or unconscionable means to collect or attempt to collect any debt. Without limiting the general application of the foregoing, the following conduct is a violation of this section:

(1) The collection of any amount (including any interest, fee, charge, or expense incidental to the principal obligation) unless such amount is expressly authorized by the agreement creating the debt or permitted by law.

(2) The acceptance by a debt collector from any person of a check or other payment instrument postdated by more than five days unless such person is notified in writing of the debt collector's intent to deposit such check or instrument not more than ten nor less than three business days prior to such deposit.

(3) The solicitation by a debt collector of any postdated check or other postdated payment instrument for the purpose of threatening or instituting criminal prosecution.

(4) Depositing or threatening to deposit any postdated check or other postdated payment instrument prior to the date on such check or instrument.

(5) Causing charges to be made to any person for communications by concealment of the true propose of the communication. Such charges include, but are not limited to, collect telephone calls and telegram fees.

(6) Taking or threatening to take any nonjudicial action to effect dispossession or disablement of property if—

(A) there is no present right to possession of the property claimed as collateral through an enforceable security interest;

(B) there is no present intention to take possession of the property; or

(C) the property is exempt by law from such dispossession or disablement.

(7) Communicating with a consumer regarding a debt by post card.

(8) Using any language or symbol, other than the debt collector's address, on any envelope when communicating with a consumer by use of the mails or by telegram, except that a debt collector

may use his business name if such name does not indicate that he is in the debt collection business.

§ 809. Validation of debts

(a) Within five days after the initial communication with a consumer in connection with the collection of any debt, a debt collector shall, unless the following information is contained in the initial communication or the consumer has paid the debt, send the consumer a written notice containing—

(1) the amount of the debt;

(2) the name of the creditor to whom the debt is owed;

(3) a statement that unless the consumer, within thirty days after receipt of the notice, disputes the validity of the debt, or any portion thereof, the debt will be assumed to be valid by the debt collector;

(4) a statement that if the consumer notifies the debt collector in writing within the thirty-day period that the debt, or any portion thereof, is disputed, the debt collector will obtain verification of the debt or a copy of a judgment against the consumer and a copy of such veri-

fication or judgment will be mailed to the consumer by the debt collector; and

(5) a statement that, upon the consumer's written request within the thirty-day period, the debt collector will provide the consumer with the name and address of the original creditor, if different from the current creditor.

(b) If the consumer notifies the debt collector in writing within the thirty-day period described in subsection (a) that the debt, or any portion thereof, is disputed, or that the consumer requests the name and address of the original creditor, the debt collector shall cease collection of the debt, or any disputed portion thereof, until the debt collector obtains verification of the debt or any copy of a judgment, or the name and address of the original creditor, and a copy of such verification or judgment, or name and address of the original creditor, is mailed to the consumer by the debt collector. Collection activities and communications that do not otherwise violate this title may continue during the 30-day period referred to in subsection (a) unless the consumer has notified the debt collector in writing that the debt, or any portion of the debt, is disputed or that the consumer requests the name and address of the original creditor. Any collection activities and communication during the 30-day period may not overshadow or be inconsistent with the disclosure of the consumer's right to dispute the debt or request the name and address of the original creditor.

(c) The failure of a consumer to dispute the validity of a debt under this section may not be construed by any court as an admission of liability by the consumer.

(d) A communication in the form of a formal pleading in a civil action shall not be treated as an initial communication for purposes of subsection (a).

(e) The sending or delivery of any form or notice which does not relate to the collection of a debt and is expressly required by the Internal Revenue Code of 1986, title V of Gramm-Leach-Bliley Act, or any provision of Federal or State law relating to notice of data security breach or privacy, or any regulation prescribed under any such provision of law, shall not be treated as an initial communication in connection with debt collection for purposes of this section.

§ 810. Multiple debts

If any consumer owes multiple debts and makes any single payment to any debt collector with respect to such debts, such debt collector may not apply such payment to any debt which is disputed by the consumer and, where applicable, shall apply such payment in accordance with the consumer's directions.

§ 811. Legal actions by debt collectors

(a) Any debt collector who brings any legal action on a debt against any consumer shall—

(1) in the case of an action to enforce an interest in real property securing the consumer's obligation, bring such action only in a judicial district or similar legal entity in which such real property is located; or

(2) in the case of an action not described in paragraph (1), bring such action only in the judicial district or similar legal entity—

(A) in which such consumer signed the contract sued upon; or

(B) in which such consumer resides at the commencement of the action.

(b) Nothing in this title shall be construed to authorize the bringing of legal actions by debt collectors.

§ 812. Furnishing certain deceptive forms

(a) It is unlawful to design, compile, and furnish any form knowing that such form would be used to create the false belief in a consumer that a person other than the creditor of such consumer is participating in the collection of or in an attempt to collect a debt such consumer allegedly owes such creditor, when in fact such person is not so participating.

(b) Any person who violates this section shall be liable to the same extent and in the same manner as a debt collector is liable under section 813 for failure to comply with a provision of this title.

§ 813. Civil liability

(a) Except as otherwise provided by this section, any debt collector who fails to comply with any provision of this title with respect to any person is liable to such person in an amount equal to the sum of—

(1) any actual damage sustained by such person as a result of such failure;

(2) (A) in the case of any action by an individual, such additional damages as the court may allow, but not exceeding $1,000; or (B) in the case of a class action,

(i) such amount for each named plaintiff as could be recovered under subparagraph (A), and

(ii) such amount as the court may allow for all other class members, without regard to a minimum individual recovery, not to exceed the lesser of $500,000 or 1 per centum of the net worth of the debt collector; and

(3) in the case of any successful action to enforce the foregoing liability, the costs of the action, together with a reasonable attorney's fee as determined by the court. On a finding by the court that an action under this section was brought in bad faith and for the purpose of harassment, the court may award to the defendant attorney's fees reasonable in relation to the work expended and costs.

(b) In determining the amount of liability in any action under subsection (a), the court shall consider, among other relevant factors—

(1) in any individual action under subsection (a) (2)(A), the frequency and persistence of noncompliance by the debt collector, the nature of such noncompliance, and the extent to which such noncompliance was intentional; or

(2) in any class action under subsection (a)(2)(B), the frequency and persistence of noncompliance by the debt collector, the nature of such noncompliance, the resources of the debt collector, the number of persons adversely affected, and the extent to which the debt collector's noncompliance was intentional.

(c) A debt collector may not be held liable in any action brought under this title if the debt collector shows by a preponderance of evidence that the violation was not intentional and resulted from a bona fide error notwithstanding the maintenance of procedures reasonably adapted to avoid any such error.

(d) An action to enforce any liability created by this title may be brought in any appropriate United States district court without regard to the amount in controversy, or in any other court of competent jurisdiction, within one year from the date on which the violation occurs.

(e) No provision of this section imposing any liability shall apply to any act done or omitted in good faith in conformity with any advisory opinion of the Commission, notwithstanding that after such act or omission has occurred, such opinion is amended, rescinded, or determined by judicial or other authority to be invalid for any reason.

§ 814. Administrative enforcement

(a) Compliance with this title shall be enforced by the Commission, except to the extent that enforcement of the requirements imposed under this title is specifically committed to another agency under subsection (b). For purpose of the exercise by the Commission of its functions and powers under the Federal Trade Commission Act, a violation of this title shall be deemed an unfair or deceptive act or practice in violation of that Act. All of the functions and powers of the Commission under the Federal Trade Commission Act are available to the Commission to enforce compliance by any person with this title, irrespective of whether that person is engaged in commerce or meets any other jurisdictional tests in the Federal Trade Commission Act, including the power to enforce the provisions of this title in the same manner as if the violation had been a violation of a Federal Trade Commission trade regulation rule.

(b) Compliance with any requirements imposed under this title shall be enforced under—

(1) section 8 of the Federal Deposit Insurance Act, in the case of—

(A) national banks, by the Comptroller of the Currency;

(B) member banks of the Federal Reserve System (other than national banks), by the Federal Reserve Board; and

(C) banks the deposits or accounts of which are insured by the Federal Deposit Insurance Corporation (other than members of the Federal Reserve System), by the Board of Directors of the Federal Deposit Insurance Corporation;

(2) section 5(d) of the Home Owners Loan Act of 1933, section 407 of the National Housing Act, and sections 6(i) and 17 of the Federal Home Loan Bank Act, by the Federal Home Loan Bank Board (acting directing or through the Federal Savings and Loan Insurance Corporation), in the case of any institution subject to any of those provisions;

(3) the Federal Credit Union Act, by the Administrator of the National Credit Union Administration with respect to any Federal credit union;

(4) subtitle IV of Title 49, by the Interstate Commerce Commission with respect to any common carrier subject to such subtitle;

(5) the Federal Aviation Act of 1958, by the Secretary of Transportation with respect to any air carrier or any foreign air carrier subject to that Act; and

(6) the Packers and Stockyards Act, 1921 (except as provided in section 406 of that Act), by the Secretary of Agriculture with respect to any activities subject to that Act.

(c) For the purpose of the exercise by any agency referred to in subsection (b) of its powers under any Act referred to in that subsection, a violation of any requirement imposed under this title shall be deemed to be a violation of a requirement imposed under that Act. In addition to its powers under any provision of law specifically referred to in subsection (b), each of the agencies referred to in that subsection may exercise, for the purpose of enforcing compliance with any requirement imposed under this title any other authority conferred on it by law, except as provided in subsection (d).

(d) Neither the Commission nor any other agency referred to in subsection (b) may promulgate trade regulation rules or other regulations with respect to the collection of debts by debt collectors as defined in this title.

§ 815. Reports to Congress by the Commission

(a) Not later than one year after the effective date of this title and at one-year intervals thereafter, the Commission shall make reports to the Congress concerning the administration of its functions under this title, including such recommendations as the Commission deems necessary or appropriate. In addition, each report of the Commission shall include its assessment of the extent to which compliance with this title is being achieved and a summary of the enforcement actions taken by the Commission under section 814 of this title.

(b) In the exercise of its functions under this title, the Commission may obtain upon request the views of any other Federal agency which exercises enforcement functions under section 814 of this title.

§ 816. Relation to State laws

This title does not annul, alter, or affect, or exempt any person subject to the provisions of this title from complying with the laws of any State with respect to debt collection practices, except to the extent that those laws are inconsistent with any provision of this title, and then only to the extent of the inconsistency. For purposes of this section, a State law is not inconsistent with this title if the protection such law affords any consumer is greater than the protection provided by this title.

§ 817. Exemption for State regulation

The Commission shall by regulation exempt from the requirements of this title any class of debt collection practices within any State if the Commission determines that under the law of that State that class of debt collection practices is subject to requirements substantially similar to those imposed by this title, and that there is adequate provision for enforcement.

§ 818. Exception for certain bad check enforcement programs operated by private entities

(a) In General.—

(1) TREATMENT OF CERTAIN PRIVATE ENTITIES.

—Subject to paragraph (2), a private entity shall be excluded from the definition of a debt collector, pursuant to the exception provided in section 803(6), with respect to the operation by the entity of a program described in paragraph (2)(A) under a contract described in paragraph (2)(B).

(2) CONDITIONS OF APPLICABILITY.

—Paragraph (1) shall apply if—

(A) a State or district attorney establishes, within the jurisdiction of such State or dis trict attorney and with respect to alleged bad check violations that do not involve a check described in subsection (b), a pretrial diversion program for alleged bad check offenders who agree to participate voluntarily in such program to avoid criminal prosecution;

(B) a private entity, that is subject to an administrative support services contract with a State or district attorney and operates under the direction, supervision, and control of such State or district attorney, operates the pretrial diversion program described in subparagraph (A); and

(C) in the course of performing duties delegated to it by a State or district attorney under the contract, the private entity referred to in subparagraph (B)—

(i) complies with the penal laws of the State;

(ii) conforms with the terms of the contract and directives of the State or district attorney;

(iii) does not exercise independent prosecutorial discretion;

(iv) contacts any alleged offender referred to in subparagraph (A) for purposes of participating in a program referred to in such paragraph—

(I) only as a result of any determination by the State or district attorney that probable cause of a bad check violation under State penal law exists, and that contact with the alleged offender for purposes of participation in the program is appropriate; and

(II) the alleged offender has failed to pay the bad check after demand for payment, pursuant to State law, is made for payment of the check amount;

(v) includes as part of an initial written communication with an alleged offender a clear and conspicuous statement that—

   (I) the alleged offender may dispute the validity of any alleged bad check violation;

   (II) where the alleged offender knows, or has reasonable cause to believe, that the alleged bad check violation is the result of theft or forgery of the check, identity theft, or other fraud that is not the result of the conduct of the alleged offender, the alleged offender may file a crime report with the appropriate law enforcement agency; and

   (III) if the alleged offender notifies the private entity or the district attorney in writing, not later than 30 days after being contacted for the first time pursuant to clause (iv), that there is a dispute pursuant to this subsection, before further restitution efforts are pursued, the district attorney or an employee of the district attorney authorized to make such a determination makes a determination that there is probable cause to believe that a crime has been committed; and

(vi) charges only fees in connection with services under the contract that have been authorized by the contract with the State or district attorney.

(b) Certain Checks Excluded.—A check is described in this subsection if the check involves, or is subsequently found to involve—

(1) a postdated check presented in connection with a pay-day loan, or other similar transaction, where the payee of the check knew that the issuer had insufficient funds at the time the check was made, drawn, or delivered;

(2) a stop payment order where the issuer acted in good faith and with reasonable cause in stopping payment on the check;

(3) a check dishonored because of an adjustment to the issuer's account by the financial institution holding such account without providing notice to the person at the time the check was made, drawn, or delivered;

(4) a check for partial payment of a debt where the payee had previously accepted partial payment for such debt;

(5) a check issued by a person who was not competent, or was not of legal age, to enter into a legal contractual obligation at the time the check was made, drawn, or delivered; or

(6) a check issued to pay an obligation arising from a transaction that was illegal in the jurisdiction of the State or district attorney at the time the check was made, drawn, or delivered.

(c) Definitions.—For purposes of this section, the following definitions shall apply:

(1) STATE OR DISTRICT ATTORNEY.—The term "State or district attorney" means the chief elected or appointed prosecuting attorney in a district, county (as defined in section 2 of title 1, United States Code), municipality, or comparable jurisdiction, including State attorneys general who act as chief elected or appointed prosecuting attorneys in a district, county (as so defined), municipality or comparable jurisdiction, who may be referred to by a variety of titles such as district attorneys, prosecuting attorneys, commonwealth's attorneys, solicitors, county attorneys, and state's attorneys, and who are responsible for the prosecution of State crimes and violations of jurisdiction-specific local ordinances.

(2) CHECK.—The term "check" has the same meaning as in section 3(6) of the Check Clearing for the 21st Century Act.

(3) BAD CHECK VIOLATION.—The term "bad check violation" means a violation of the applicable State criminal law relating to the writing of dishonored checks.

§ 819. Effective date

This title takes effect upon the expiration of six months after the date of its enactment, but section 809 shall apply only with respect to debts for which the initial attempt to collect occurs after such effective date.

Appendix D
Gramm-Leach-Bliley Act

The Gramm-Leach-Bliley Act is also known as the Financial Services Modernization Act of 1999. This law is so broad in scope that I have only given you the part of the law that pertains to pretexting and to you as a skip tracer. To sum this up in a few sentences: it means that you are not allowed to lie to a financial institution when you are skip tracing and gathering information. This law did not make bank levies illegal. Subpoenas are still legal. When contacting a financial institution, make sure to tell the truth, and then you will not be breaking the law.

TITLE V—PRIVACY

Subtitle A—Disclosure of Nonpublic Personal Information

SEC. 501. PROTECTION OF NONPUBLIC PERSONAL INFORMATION

(a) PRIVACY OBLIGATION POLICY.—It is the policy of the Congress that each financial institution has an affirmative and continuing obligation to respect the privacy of its customers and to protect the security and confidentiality of those customers' nonpublic personal information.

(b) FINANCIAL INSTITUTIONS SAFEGUARDS.—In furtherance of the policy in subsection (a), each agency or authority described in section 505(a) shall establish appropriate standards for the financial institutions subject to their jurisdiction relating to administrative, technical, and physical safeguards

(1) to insure the security and confidentiality of customer records and information;

(2) to protect against any anticipated threats or hazards to the security or integrity of such records and

(3) to protect against unauthorized access to or use of such records or information which could result in substantial harm or inconvenience to any customer.

SEC. 502. OBLIGATIONS WITH RESPECT TO DISCLOSURES OF PERSONAL INFORMATION.

(a) NOTICE REQUIREMENTS.—Except as otherwise provided in this subtitle, a financial institution may not, directly or through any affiliate, disclose to a nonaffiliated third party any nonpublic personal information, unless such financial institution provides or has provided to the consumer a notice that complies with section 503. 10

(b) OPT OUT.—

(1) IN GENERAL.—A financial institution may not disclose nonpublic personal information to a nonaffiliated third party unless—

(A) such financial institution clearly and conspicuously discloses to the consumer, in writing or in electronic form or other form permitted by the regulations prescribed under section 504, that such information may be disclosed to such third party;

(B) the consumer is given the opportunity, before the time that such information is initially disclosed, to direct that such information not be disclosed to such third party; and

(C) the consumer is given an explanation of how the consumer can exercise that non-disclosure option.

(2) EXCEPTION.—This subsection shall not prevent a financial institution from providing nonpublic personal information to a nonaffiliated third party to perform services for or functions on

behalf of the financial institution, including marketing of the financial institution's own products or services, or financial products or services offered pursuant to joint agreements between two or more financial institutions that comply with the requirements imposed by the regulations prescribed under section 504, if the financial institution fully discloses the pro- viding of such information and enters into a contractual agreement with the third party that requires the third party to maintain the confidentiality of such information.

(c) LIMITS ON REUSE OF INFORMATION.—Except as otherwise provided in this subtitle, a nonaffiliated third party that receives from a financial institution nonpublic personal information under this section shall not, directly or through an affiliate of such receiving third party, disclose such information to any other person that is a non-affiliated third party of both the financial institution and such receiving third party, unless such disclosure would be lawful if made directly to such other person by the financial institution.

(d) LIMITATIONS ON THE SHARING OF ACCOUNT NUMBER INFORMATION FOR MARKETING PURPOSES.—A financial institution shall not disclose, other than to a consumer reporting agency, an account number or similar form of access number or access code for a credit card account, deposit account, or transaction account of a consumer to any nonaffiliated third party for use in telemarketing, direct mail marketing, or other marketing through electronic mail to the consumer.

(e) GENERAL EXCEPTIONS.—Subsections (a) and (b) shall not prohibit the disclosure of nonpublic personal information—

(1) as necessary to effect, administer, or enforce a transaction requested or authorized by the consumer, or in connection with

(A) servicing or processing a financial product or service requested or authorized by the consumer;

(B) maintaining or servicing the consumer's account with the financial institution, or with another entity as part of a private label credit card program or other extension of credit on behalf of such entity; or

(C) a proposed or actual securitization, secondary market sale (including sales of servicing rights), or similar transaction related to a transaction of the consumer;

(2) with the consent or at the direction of the consumer;

(3) (A) to protect the confidentiality or security of the financial institution's records pertaining to

the consumer, the service or product, or the transaction therein; (B) to protect against or prevent actual or potential fraud, unauthorized transactions, claims, or other liability; (C) for required institutional risk control, or for resolving customer disputes or inquiries; (D) to persons holding a legal or beneficial interest relating to the consumer; or (E) to persons acting in a fiduciary or representative capacity on behalf of the consumer;

(4) to provide information to insurance rate advisory organizations, guaranty funds or agencies, applicable rating agencies of the financial institution, persons assessing the institution's compliance with industry standards, and the institution's attorneys, accountants, and auditors;

(5) to the extent specifically permitted or required under other provisions of law and in accordance with the Right to Financial Privacy Act of 1978, to law enforcement agencies (including a Federal functional regulator, the Secretary of the Treasury with respect to subchapter II of chapter 53 of title 31, United States Code, and chapter 2 of title I of Public Law 91–508 (12 U.S.C. 1951–1959), a State insurance authority, or the Federal Trade Commission), self-regulatory organizations, or for an investigation on a matter related to public safety;

(6) (A) to a consumer reporting agency in accordance with the Fair Credit Reporting Act, or (B) from a consumer report reported by a consumer reporting agency;

(7) in connection with a proposed or actual sale, merger, transfer, or exchange of all or a portion of a business or operating unit if the disclosure of nonpublic personal information concerns solely consumers of such business or unit; or

(8) to comply with Federal, State, or local laws, rules, and other applicable legal requirements; to comply with a properly authorized civil, criminal, or regulatory investigation or subpoena or summons by Federal, State, or local authorities; or to respond to judicial process or government regulatory authorities having jurisdiction over the financial institution for examination, compliance, or other purposes as authorized by law.

SEC. 503. DISCLOSURE OF INSTITUTION PRIVACY POLICY.

(a) DISCLOSURE REQUIRED.—At the time of establishing a customer relationship with a consumer and not less than annually during the continuation of such relationship, a financial institution shall provide a clear and conspicuous disclosure to such consumer, in writing or in electronic form or other form permitted by the regulations prescribed under section 504, of such financial institution's policies and practices with respect to

(1) disclosing nonpublic personal information to affiliates and nonaffiliated third parties, consistent with section 502, including the categories of information that may be disclosed;

(2) disclosing nonpublic personal information of persons who have ceased to be customers of the financial institution; and

(3) protecting the nonpublic personal information of consumers. Such disclosures shall be made in accordance with the regulations prescribed under section 504.

(b) INFORMATION TO BE INCLUDED.—The disclosure required by subsection (a) shall include—

(1) the policies and practices of the institution with respect to disclosing nonpublic personal information to nonaffiliated third parties, other than agents of the institution, consistent with section 502 of this subtitle, and including—

(A) the categories of persons to whom the information is or may be disclosed, other than the persons to whom the information may be provided pursuant to section 502(e); and

(B) the policies and practices of the institution with respect to disclosing of nonpublic personal information of persons who have

ceased to be customers of the financial institution;

(2) the categories of nonpublic personal information that are collected by the financial institution;

(3) the policies that the institution maintains to
protect the confidentiality and security of nonpublic personal information in accordance
with section 501; and

(4) the disclosures required, if any, under section
603(d)(2)(A)(iii) of the Fair Credit Reporting
Act.

SEC. 504. RULEMAKING.

(a) REGULATORY AUTHORITY.—

(1) RULEMAKING.—The Federal banking agencies,
the National Credit Union Administration, the
Secretary of the Treasury, the Securities and
Exchange Commission, and the Federal Trade
Commission shall each prescribe, after consultation as appropriate with representatives
of State insurance authorities designated by
the National Association of Insurance Commissioners, such regulations as may be necessary to carry out the purposes of this subtitle
with respect to the financial institutions subject
to their jurisdiction under section 505.

(2) COORDINATION, CONSISTENCY, AND COMPARABILITY.—Each of the agencies and authorities required under paragraph (1) to prescribe regulations shall consult and coordinate with the other such agencies and authorities for the purposes of assuring, to the extent possible, that the regulations prescribed by each such agency and authority are consistent and comparable with the regulations prescribed by the other such agencies and authorities.

(3) PROCEDURES AND DEADLINE.—Such regulations shall be prescribed in accordance with applicable requirements of title 5, United States Code, and shall be issued in final form not later than 6 months after the date of the enactment of this Act.

(b) AUTHORITY TO GRANT EXCEPTIONS.—The regulations prescribed under subsection (a) may include such additional exceptions to subsections (a) through (d) of section 502 as are deemed consistent with the purposes of this subtitle.

SEC. 505. ENFORCEMENT.

(a) IN GENERAL.—This subtitle and the regulations prescribed thereunder shall be enforced by the Federal functional regulators, the State insurance authorities, and the Federal Trade Commission with respect to financial institutions and other persons subject to their jurisdiction under applicable law, as follows:

(1) Under section 8 of the Federal Deposit Insurance Act, in the case of

(A) national banks, Federal branches and Federal agencies of foreign banks, and any subsidiaries of such entities (except brokers, dealers, persons providing insurance, investment companies, and investment advisers), by the Office of the Comptroller of the Currency;

(B) member banks of the Federal Reserve System (other than national banks), branches and agencies of foreign banks (other than Federal branches, Federal agencies, and insured State branches of foreign banks), commercial lending companies owned or controlled by foreign banks, organizations operating under section 25 or 25A of the Federal Reserve Act, and bank holding companies and their nonbank subsidiaries or affiliates (except brokers, dealers, persons providing insurance, investment companies, and investment advisers), by the Board of Governors of the Federal Reserve System;

(C) banks insured by the Federal Deposit Insurance Corporation (other than members of the Federal Reserve System), insured State branches of foreign banks, and any sub-sidiaries of such entities (except brokers, dealers, persons providing insurance, investment companies, and investment advisers), by the Board of Directors of the Federal Deposit Insurance Corporation; and

(D) savings associations the deposits of which are insured by the Federal Deposit Insurance Corporation, and any subsidiaries of such savings associations (except brokers, dealers, persons providing insurance, investment companies, and investment advisers), by the Director of the Office of Thrift Supervision.

(2) Under the Federal Credit Union Act, by the Board of the National Credit Union Administration with respect to any federally insured credit union, and any subsidiaries of such an entity.

(3) Under the Securities Exchange Act of 1934, by the Securities and Exchange Commission with respect to any broker or dealer.

(4) Under the Investment Company Act of 1940, by the Securities and Exchange Commission with respect to investment companies.

(5) Under the Investment Advisers Act of 1940, by the Securities and Exchange Commission with

respect to investment advisers registered with the Commission under such Act.

(6) Under State insurance law, in the case of any person engaged in providing insurance, by the applicable State insurance authority of the State in which the person is domiciled, subject to section 104 of this Act.

(7) Under the Federal Trade Commission Act, by the Federal Trade Commission for any other financial institution or other person that is not subject to the jurisdiction of any agency or authority under paragraphs (1) through (6) of this subsection.

(b) ENFORCEMENT OF SECTION 501.—

(1) IN GENERAL.—Except as provided in paragraph (2), the agencies and authorities described in subsection (a) shall implement the standards prescribed under section 501(b) in the same manner, to the extent practicable, as standards prescribed pursuant to section 39(a) of the Federal Deposit Insurance Act are implemented pursuant to such section.

(2) EXCEPTION.—The agencies and authorities described in paragraphs (3), (4), (5), (6), and (7) of subsection (a) shall implement the standards prescribed under section 501(b) by rule with respect to the financial institutions and

other persons subject to their respective juris-dictions under subsection (a).

(c) ABSENCE OF STATE ACTION.—If a State insurance authority fails to adopt regulations to carry out this subtitle, such State shall not be eligible to override, pursuant to section 45(g)(2)(B)(iii) of the Federal Deposit Insurance Act, the insurance customer protection regulations prescribed by a Federal banking agency under section 45(a) of such Act.

(d) DEFINITIONS.—The terms used in subsection (a)(1) that are not defined in this subtitle or otherwise defined in section 3(s) of the Federal Deposit Insurance Act shall have the same meaning as given in section 1(b) of the International Banking Act of 1978.

SEC. 506. PROTECTION OF FAIR CREDIT REPORTING ACT.

(a) AMENDMENT.—Section 621 of the Fair Credit Reporting Act (15 U.S.C. 1681s) is amended

(1) in subsection (d), by striking everything follow-ing the end of the second sentence; and

(2) by striking subsection (e) and inserting the fol-lowing:

"(e) REGULATORY AUTHORITY.—

"(1) The Federal banking agencies referred to in paragraphs (1) and (2) of subsection (b) shall jointly prescribe such regulations as necessary to carry out the purposes of this Act with respect to any persons identified under paragraphs (1) and (2) of subsection (b), and the Board of Governors of the Federal Reserve System shall have authority to prescribe regulations consistent with such joint regulations with respect to bank holding companies and affiliates (other than depository institutions and consumer reporting agencies) of such holding companies.

"(2) The Board of the National Credit Union Administration shall prescribe such regulations as necessary to carry out the purposes of this Act with respect to any persons identified under paragraph (3) of subsection (b).".

(b) CONFORMING AMENDMENT.—Section 621(a) of the Fair Credit Reporting Act (15 U.S.C. 1681s(a)) is amended by striking paragraph (4).

(c) RELATION TO OTHER PROVISIONS.—Except for the amendments made by subsections (a) and (b), nothing in this title shall be construed to modify, limit, or supersede the operation of the Fair Credit Reporting Act, and no inference shall be drawn on the basis of the provisions of this title regarding whether information is transaction or experience information under section 603 of such Act.

SEC. 507. RELATION TO STATE LAWS.

(a) IN GENERAL.—This subtitle and the amendments made by this subtitle shall not be construed as superseding, altering, or affecting any statute, regulation, order, or interpretation in effect in any State, except to the extent that such statute, regulation, order, or interpretation is inconsistent with the provisions of this subtitle, and then only to the extent of the inconsistency.

(b) GREATER PROTECTION UNDER STATE LAW.— For purposes of this section, a State statute, regulation, order, or interpretation is not inconsistent with the provisions of this subtitle if the protection such statute, regulation, order, or interpretation affords any person is greater than the protection provided under this subtitle and the amendments made by this subtitle, as determined by the Federal Trade Commission, after consultation with the agency or authority with jurisdiction under section 505(a) of either the person that initiated the complaint or that is the subject of the complaint, on its own motion or upon the petition of any interested party.

SEC. 508. STUDY OF INFORMATION SHARING AMONG FINANCIAL AFFILIATES.

(a) IN GENERAL.—The Secretary of the Treasury, in conjunction with the Federal functional regulators and the Federal Trade Commission, shall conduct a study of information sharing practices among financial institutions and their affiliates. Such study shall include—

(1) the purposes for the sharing of confidential customer information with affiliates or with non-affiliated third parties;

(2) the extent and adequacy of security protections for such information;

(3) the potential risks for customer privacy of such sharing of information;

(4) the potential benefits for financial institutions and affiliates of such sharing of information;

(5) the potential benefits for customers of such sharing of information;

(6) the adequacy of existing laws to protect customer privacy;

(7) the adequacy of financial institution privacy policy and privacy rights disclosure under existing law;

(8) the feasibility of different approaches, including opt-out and opt-in, to permit customers to direct that confidential information not be shared with affiliates and nonaffiliated third parties; and

(9) the feasibility of restricting sharing of information for specific uses or of permitting customers to direct the uses for which information may be shared.

(b) CONSULTATION.—The Secretary shall consult with representatives of State insurance authorities designated by the National Association of Insurance Commissioners, and also with financial services industry, consumer organizations and privacy groups, and other representatives of the general public, in formulating and conducting the study required by subsection (a).

(c) REPORT.—On or before January 1, 2002, the Secretary shall submit a report to the Congress containing the findings and conclusions of the study required under subsection (a), together with such recommendations for legislative or administrative action as may be appropriate.

SEC. 509. DEFINITIONS.

As used in this subtitle:

    (1) FEDERAL BANKING AGENCY.—The term "Federal banking agency" has the same meaning as given in section 3 of the Federal Deposit Insurance Act.

    (2) FEDERAL FUNCTIONAL REGULATOR.—The term "Federal functional regulator" means—

        (A) the Board of Governors of the Federal Reserve System;

        (B) the Office of the Comptroller of the Currency;

        (C) the Board of Directors of the Federal Deposit Insurance Corporation;

        (D) the Director of the Office of Thrift Supervision;

        (E) the National Credit Union Administration Board; and

        (F) the Securities and Exchange Commission.

    (3) FINANCIAL INSTITUTION.—

(A) IN GENERAL.—The term "financial institution" means any institution the business of which is engaging in financial activities as described in section 4(k) of the Bank Holding Company Act of 1956.

(B) PERSONS SUBJECT TO CFTC REGULATION.—Notwithstanding subparagraph (A), the term "financial institution" does not include any person or entity with respect to any financial activity that is subject to the jurisdiction of the Commodity Futures Trading Commission under the Commodity Exchange Act.

(C) FARM CREDIT INSTITUTIONS.—Notwithstanding subparagraph (A), the term "financial institution" does not include the Federal Agricultural Mortgage Corporation or any entity chartered and operating under the Farm Credit Act of 1971.

(D) OTHER SECONDARY MARKET INSTITUTIONS.—Notwithstanding subparagraph (A), the term "financial institution" does not include institutions chartered by Congress specifically to engage in transactions described in section 502(e)(1)(C), as long as such institutions do not sell or transfer nonpublic personal information to a nonaffiliated third party.

(4) NONPUBLIC PERSONAL INFORMATION.—

(A) The term "nonpublic personal information" means personally identifiable financial information—

(i) provided by a consumer to a financial institution;

(ii) resulting from any transaction with the consumer or any service per- formed for the consumer; or

(iii) otherwise obtained by the financial institution.

(B) Such term does not include publicly available information, as such term is defined by the regulations prescribed under section 504.

(C) Notwithstanding subparagraph (B), such term—

(i) shall include any list, description, or other grouping of consumers (and publicly available information pertaining to them) that is derived using any nonpublic personal information other than publicly available information; but

(ii) shall not include any list, description, or other grouping of consumers (and publicly available information pertaining to them) that is derived without using any nonpublic personal information.

(5) NONAFFILIATED THIRD PARTY.—The term "nonaffiliated third party" means any entity that is not an affiliate of, or related by common ownership or affiliated by corporate control with, the financial institution, but does not include a joint employee of such institution.

(6) AFFILIATE.—The term "affiliate" means any company that controls, is controlled by, or is under common control with another company.

(7) NECESSARY TO EFFECT, ADMINISTER, OR ENFORCE.—The term "as necessary to effect, administer, or enforce the transaction" means—

(A) the disclosure is required, or is a usual, appropriate, or acceptable method, to carry out the transaction or the product or service business of which the transaction is a part, and record or service or maintain the consumer's account in the ordinary course of providing the financial service or financial product, or to administer or service benefits or claims relating to the transaction or the product or service business of which it is a part, and includes—

(i) providing the consumer or the consumer's agent or broker with a confirmation, statement, or other record of the transaction, or information on the status or value of the financial service or financial product; and

(ii) the accrual or recognition of incentives or bonuses associated with the transaction that are provided by the financial institution or any other party;

(B) the disclosure is required, or is one of the lawful or appropriate methods, to enforce the rights of the financial institution or of other persons engaged in carrying out the financial transaction, or providing the product or service;

(C) the disclosure is required, or is a usual, appropriate, or acceptable method, for insurance underwriting at the consumer's request or for reinsurance purposes, or for any of the following purposes as they relate to a consumer's insurance: account administration, reporting, investigating, or preventing fraud or material misrepresentation, processing premium payments, processing insurance claims, administering insurance benefits (including utilization review activities), participating in research projects, or as otherwise required or specifically permitted by Federal or State law; or

(D) the disclosure is required, or is a usual, appropriate or acceptable method, in connection with—

(i) the authorization, settlement, billing, processing, clearing, transferring, reconciling, or collection of amounts charged, debited, or otherwise paid using a debit, credit or other payment card, check, or account number, or by other payment means;

(ii) the transfer of receivables, accounts or interests therein; or

(iii) the audit of debit, credit or other payment information.

(8) STATE INSURANCE AUTHORITY.—The term "State insurance authority" means, in the case of any person engaged in providing insurance, the State insurance authority of the State in which the person is domiciled.

(9) CONSUMER.—The term "consumer" means an individual who obtains, from a financial institution, financial products or services which are to be used primarily for personal, family, or household purposes, and also means the legal representative of such an individual.

(10) JOINT AGREEMENT.—The term "joint agreement" means a formal written contract pursuant to which two or more financial institutions jointly offer, endorse, or sponsor a financial product or service, and as may be further defined in the regulations prescribed under section 504.

(11) CUSTOMER RELATIONSHIP.—The term "time of establishing a customer relationship" shall be defined by the regulations prescribed under section 504, and shall, in the case of a financial institution engaged in extending credit directly to consumers to finance purchases of goods or services, mean the time of establishing the credit relationship with the consumer.

SEC. 510. EFFECTIVE DATE.

This subtitle shall take effect 6 months after the date on which rules are required to be prescribed under section 504(a)(3), except— (1) to the extent that a later date is specified in the rules prescribed under section 504; and (2) that sections 504 and 506 shall be effective upon enactment.

Subtitle B—Fraudulent Access to Financial Information

SEC. 521. PRIVACY PROTECTION FOR CUSTOMER INFORMATION OF FINANCIAL INSTITUTIONS.

(a) PROHIBITION ON OBTAINING CUSTOMER INFORMATION BY FALSE PRETENSES.—It shall be a violation of this subtitle for any person to obtain or attempt to obtain, or cause to be disclosed or attempt to cause to be disclosed to any person, customer information of a financial institution relating to another person—

(1) by making a false, fictitious, or fraudulent statement or representation to an officer, employee, or agent of a financial institution;

(2) by making a false, fictitious, or fraudulent statement or representation to a customer of a financial institution; or

(3) by providing any document to an officer, employee, or agent of a financial institution, knowing that the document is forged, counterfeit, lost, or stolen, was fraudulently obtained, or contains a false, fictitious, or fraudulent statement or representation.

(b) PROHIBITION ON SOLICITATION OF A PERSON TO OBTAIN CUSTOMER INFORMATION FROM FINANCIAL INSTITUTION UNDER FALSE PRETENSES.—It shall be a violation of this subtitle to request a person to obtain customer information of a financial institution, knowing that the person will obtain, or attempt to obtain, the information from the institution in any manner described in subsection (a).

(c) NONAPPLICABILITY TO LAW ENFORCEMENT AGENCIES.—No provision of this section shall be construed so as to prevent any action by a law enforcement agency, or any officer, employee, or agent of such agency, to obtain customer information of a financial institution in connection with the performance of the official duties of the agency.

(d) NONAPPLICABILITY TO FINANCIAL INSTITUTIONS IN CERTAIN CASES.—No provision of this section shall be construed so as to prevent any financial institution, or any officer, employee, or agent of a financial institution, from obtaining customer information of such financial institution in the course of—

(1) testing the security procedures or systems of such institution for maintaining the confidentiality of customer information;

(2) investigating allegations of misconduct or negligence on the part of any officer, employee, or agent of the financial institution; or

(3) recovering customer information of the financial institution which was obtained or received by another person in any manner described in subsection (a) or (b).

(e) NONAPPLICABILITY TO INSURANCE INSTITUTIONS FOR INVESTIGATION OF INSURANCE FRAUD.—No provision of this section shall be construed so as to prevent any insurance institution, or any officer, employee, or agency of an insurance institution, from obtaining information as part of an insurance investigation into criminal activity, fraud, material misrepresentation, or material nondisclosure that is authorized for such institution under State law, regulation, interpretation, or order.

(f) NONAPPLICABILITY TO CERTAIN TYPES OF CUSTOMER INFORMATION OF FINANCIAL INSTITUTIONS.—No provision of this section shall be construed so as to prevent any person from obtaining customer information of a financial institution that otherwise is available as a public record filed pursuant to the securities laws (as defined in section 3(a)(47) of the Securities Exchange Act of 1934).

(g) NONAPPLICABILITY TO COLLECTION OF CHILD SUPPORT JUDGMENTS.—No provision of this section shall be construed to prevent any State-licensed private investigator, or any officer, employee, or agent of such private investigator, from obtaining customer information of a financial institution, to the extent reasonably necessary to collect child support from a person adjudged to have been delinquent in his or her obligations by a Federal or State court, and to the extent that such action by a State-licensed private investigator is not unlawful under any other Federal or State law or regulation, and has been authorized by an order or judgment of a court of competent jurisdiction.

SEC. 522. ADMINISTRATIVE ENFORCEMENT.

(a) ENFORCEMENT BY FEDERAL TRADE COMMISSION.—
Except as provided in subsection (b), compliance
with this subtitle shall be enforced by the Federal
Trade Commission in the same manner and with
the same power and authority as the Commission
has under the Fair Debt Collection Practices Act to
enforce compliance with such Act.

(b) ENFORCEMENT BY OTHER AGENCIES IN CERTAIN
CASES.—

(1) IN GENERAL.—Compliance with this subtitle
shall be enforced under—

(A) section 8 of the Federal Deposit Insurance
Act, in the case of

(i) national banks, and Federal Branches
and Federal agencies of foreign banks,
by the Office of the Comptroller of the
Currency;

(ii) member banks of the Federal Reserve
System (other than national banks),
branches and agencies of foreign banks
(other than Federal branches, Federal
agencies, and insured State branches
of foreign banks), commercial lending
companies owned or controlled by foreign banks, and organizations operat-

ing under section 25 or 25A of the Federal Reserve Act, by the Board;

(iii) banks insured by the Federal Deposit Insurance Corporation (other than members of the Federal Reserve System and national nonmember banks) and insured State branches of foreign banks, by the Board of Directors of the Federal Deposit Insurance Corporation; and

(iv) savings associations the deposits of which are insured by the Federal Deposit Insurance Corporation, by the Director of the Office of Thrift Supervision; and

(B) the Federal Credit Union Act, by the Administrator of the National Credit Union Administration with respect to any Federal credit union.

(2) VIOLATIONS OF THIS SUBTITLE TREATED AS VIOLATIONS OF OTHER LAWS.—For the purpose of the exercise by any agency referred to in paragraph (1) of its powers under any Act referred to in that paragraph, a violation of this subtitle shall be deemed to be a violation of a requirement imposed under that Act. In addition to its powers under any provision of law specifically referred to in paragraph (1), each of the agencies referred to in that paragraph may exercise, for the purpose of enforcing compliance

with this subtitle, any other authority conferred on such agency by law.

SEC. 523. CRIMINAL PENALTY.

(a) IN GENERAL.—Whoever knowingly and intentionally violates, or knowingly and intentionally attempts to violate, section 521 shall be fined in accordance with title 18, United States Code, or imprisoned for not more than 5 years, or both.

(b) ENHANCED PENALTY FOR AGGRAVATED CASES.— Whoever violates, or attempts to violate, section 521 while violating another law of the United States or as part of a pattern of any illegal activity involving more than $100,000 in a 12-month period shall be fined twice the amount provided in subsection (b) (3) or (c)(3) (as the case may be) of section 3571 of title 18, United States Code, imprisoned for not more than 10 years, or both.

SEC. 524. RELATION TO STATE LAWS.

(a) IN GENERAL.—This subtitle shall not be construed as superseding, altering, or affecting the statutes, regulations, orders, or interpretations in effect in any State, except to the extent that such statutes, regulations, orders, or interpretations are inconsistent with the provisions of this subtitle, and then only to the extent of the inconsistency.

(b) GREATER PROTECTION UNDER STATE LAW.— For purposes of this section, a State statute, regulation, order, or interpretation is not inconsistent with the provisions of this subtitle if the protection such statute, regulation, order, or interpretation affords any person is greater than the protection provided under this subtitle as determined by the Federal Trade Commission, after consultation with the agency or authority with jurisdiction under section 522 of either the person that initiated the complaint or that is the subject of the complaint, on its own motion or upon the petition of any interested party.

SEC. 525. AGENCY GUIDANCE.

In furtherance of the objectives of this subtitle, each Federal banking agency (as defined in section 3(z) of the Federal Deposit Insurance Act), the National Credit Union Administration, and the Securities and Exchange Commission or self-regulatory organizations, as appropriate, shall review regulations and guidelines applicable to financial institutions under their respective jurisdictions and shall prescribe such revisions to such regulations and guidelines as may be necessary to ensure that such financial institutions have policies, procedures, and controls in place to prevent the unauthorized disclosure of customer financial information and to deter and detect activities proscribed under section 521.

SEC. 526. REPORTS.

(a) REPORT TO THE CONGRESS.—Before the end of the 18-month period beginning on the date of the enactment of this Act, the Comptroller General, in consultation with the Federal Trade Commission, Federal banking agencies, the National Credit Union Administration, the Securities and Exchange Commission, appropriate Federal law enforcement agencies, and appropriate State insurance regulators, shall submit to the Congress a report on the following:

(1) The efficacy and adequacy of the remedies provided in this subtitle in addressing attempts to obtain financial information by fraudulent means or by false pretenses.

(2) Any recommendations for additional legislative or regulatory action to address threats to the privacy of financial information created by attempts to obtain information by fraudulent means or false pretenses.

(b) ANNUAL REPORT BY ADMINISTERING AGENCIES.— The Federal Trade Commission and the Attorney General shall submit to Congress an annual report on number and disposition of all enforcement actions taken pursuant to this subtitle.

SEC. 527. DEFINITIONS.

For purposes of this subtitle, the following definitions shall apply:

(1) CUSTOMER.—The term "customer" means, with respect to a financial institution, any person (or authorized representative of a person) to whom the financial institution provides a product or service, including that of acting as a fiduciary.

(2) CUSTOMER INFORMATION OF A FINANCIAL INSTITUTION.—The term "customer information of a financial institution" means any information maintained by or for a financial institution which is derived from the relationship between the financial institution and a customer of the financial institution and is identified with the customer.

(3) DOCUMENT.—The term "document" means any information in any form.

(4) FINANCIAL INSTITUTION.—

(A) IN GENERAL.—The term "financial institution" means any institution engaged in the business of providing financial services to customers who maintain a credit, deposit, trust, or other financial account or relationship with the institution.

(B) CERTAIN FINANCIAL INSTITUTIONS SPECIFI-CALLY INCLUDED.—The term "financial institution" includes any depository institution (as defined in section 19(b)(1)(A) of the Federal Reserve Act), any broker or dealer, any investment adviser or investment company, any insurance company, any loan or finance company, any credit card issuer or operator of a credit card system, and any consumer reporting agency that compiles and maintains files on consumers on a nationwide basis (as defined in section 603(p) of the Consumer Credit Protection Act).

(C) SECURITIES INSTITUTIONS.—For purposes of subparagraph (B)—

(i) the terms "broker" and "dealer" have the same meanings as given in section 3 of the Securities Exchange Act of 1934 (15 U.S.C. 78c);

(ii) the term "investment adviser" has the same meaning as given in section 202(a)(11) of the Investment Advisers Act of 1940 (15 U.S.C. 80b–2(a)); and

(iii) the term "investment company" has the same meaning as given in section 3 of the Investment Company Act of 1940 (15 U.S.C. 80a–3).

(D) CERTAIN PERSONS AND ENTITIES SPECIFICAL-
LY EXCLUDED.—The term "financial institution" does not include any person or entity
with respect to any financial activity that is
subject to the jurisdiction of the Commodity Futures Trading Commission under the
Commodity Exchange Act and does not
include the Federal Agricultural Mortgage
Corporation or any entity chartered and
operating under the Farm Credit Act of
1971.

(E) FURTHER DEFINITION BY REGULATION.—The
Federal Trade Commission, after consultation with Federal banking agencies and
the Securities and Exchange Commission,
may prescribe regulations clarifying or de-
scribing the types of institutions which shall
be treated as financial institutions for purposes of this subtitle.

Acknowledgments

First, I must thank the National Business Institute and Pam Bjork for having motivated me to teach a class in a new and forbidden area. And for the students who allowed me to make mistakes and learn from those mistakes to make the next class a better one. And to all my students who continue to attend these seminars and ask great questions that make me think deeper.

To the PSIA, Professional Ski Instructors of America, and their president, Ray Allard, for being the coach's coach, who has helped to make me who I am. For helping to build my self-confidence and for guiding me to see teaching as a path to fulfillment. There are very few things in life that are as rewarding as seeing your students grow as a result of what they were able to learn from me. The progress has made me so happy.

To Queens College City University of New York and Dr. Joel G. Siegel, CPA, PhD, for having given me my first opportunity to coauthor a book and get a sneak peek into the world of publishing. I owe him a special gratitude for making me see the world in a different light. He is one of those professors who touch people's lives in a very special way. He made me realize that the discipline of accounting is the most important because it teaches you how to evaluate every business and every business industry from a new perspective. It is the objective nature of the discipline that makes you step aside and go above and beyond and be a complete outsider in order to make an accurate assessment.

To David Zeldin for having sponsored me for my Certified Fraud Examiners membership, which became so important because it determined what was important and what I stood for.

To John Potts and my publisher for helping me to make this edition bigger and better and teaching me every step of the way that nothing we achieve in this world is achieved alone. It is always achieved with others teaching us along the way. Also to my editors, who made me an author instead of just a writer by showing me how to put my thoughts together in an organized form.

To Greg Wittmer and Tonic Couture for having helped me with the audio book version, and for going above and beyond the call of duty. It could not have happened without you. The final job of the teacher is to free the student of the teacher.

To my competition for making me stronger and forcing me to learn from my mistakes.

To all those of you who have given me so much behind the scenes. I am so grateful to you for having me in your life. Especially to those who didn't want to be mentioned.

Index

conditional approval, 161

confidential, 206

consumer information protection, 339-345

Consumer Protection Bureau (CPB), 50

consumer reporting agencies, 165

consumer statement, to credit reports, 165

contingency basis, working on, 75

convenient skips, 6

conveyance, 149

Corporate Directory, 204

corporate privilege, abuse of, 29

corporate searches, 224-228

corporate veil, piercing, 28-29

Corporate Information, Web site, 224

corporations, merging, 30

corporations vs. individuals, skip tracing, 27-28

county clerk's office, 121

Crain Communications, Web site, 237

Credit Bureau Reports, 120

credit card charge-offs, 10

credit card "skims," 36

credit theft, 41

creditor priority, 60-62

Credit.net, Web site, 224

cyber attacks, 190

cyber passwords, 190

cyber scams, 188

cyber technology, 186

cyber terrorism, 125

cyber tracking, 125, 185

cyberspace, 125

D

data, 97-99

databank, 33

databases, 203-206

debt buyer skips, 10

debt collection

reasons court allows, 28-29

third party communication and, 312-313

debt disclosure, to third party, 75

debtor examination, 52

debtor skips, 11, 19-23

deceptive practices, 74-75

deed, 48-49, 150, 164

deep web, definition of, 183

default, 47-51, 92

default syntax, 176